Activities

for
school-age
child
care

Revised Edition

Barbara Blakley
Rosalie Blau
Elizabeth H. Brady
Catherine Streibert
Ann Zavitkovsky
Docia Zavitkovsky

Playing and Learning

National Association for the Education of Young Children, Washington, DC 20009

This revised edition is dedicated to the memory of Catherine Streibert, who used the first edition in her work with children in Santa Monica, California, and who contributed many of the ideas that have become part of this volume.

Photographs by

Jean Berlfein
5, 6, 14, 18, 42, 55, 73, 86

Barbara Brockmann
64

David Cler
46

Gail Ellison
60

Rose C. Engel
75

Lucy Fein
24

Ellen Galinsky
47

Marietta Lynch
28

Susan May
26

Esther Mugar
2, 13

Cheryl Namkung
32

David Phillips
17

Mary Ellen Powers
40, 57

James Seligman
56

Strix Pix
44

Subjects & Predicates
34, 78

Francis Wardle
59

Diane Wasserman
21, 50, 52, 53, 62

Thomas Williams
70

Illustrations by
Caroline Taylor

Second printing, 1991.

National Association for the Education of Young Children
1834 Connecticut Avenue, N.W.
Washington, DC 20009

The National Association for the Education of Young Children attempts through its publications program to provide a forum for discussion of major issues and ideas in our field. We hope to provoke thought and promote professional growth. The views expressed or implied are not necessarily those of the Association.

Library of Congress Catalog Card Number: 89-060449
ISBN Catalog Number: 0-935989-26-9
NAEYC #214
Printed in the United States of America.

Authors

Barbara Blakley
Early Childhood Specialist, Los Angeles Unified School District, California.

Rosalie Blau
Consultant, Early Childhood Education Programs, San Pablo, California.

Elizabeth H. Brady
Professor of Educational Psychology, California State University, Northridge.

Catherine Streibert
Former School-Age Child Development Coordinator,
Santa Monica Unified Schools, California.

Ann Zavitkovsky
Save the Children, Atlanta, Georgia.

Docia Zavitkovsky
Early Childhood Specialist, Los Angeles, California.

Preface

The Office of Child Development (OCD) and the Office of Economic Opportunity (OEO) grant #H–9807, through Research for Better Schools, Ronald K. Parker, Principal Investigator, provided financial support in 1970 for developing a daily activity program for 5- to 10-year-old children. The opinions expressed in the manuscript did not necessarily reflect the position or policy of OCD or OEO, and no official endorsement by these agencies should be inferred.

The original manuscript was expanded, enriched, and revised in 1977 and 1988 to increase its relevance and usefulness to those living and working creatively with school-age children in day care programs.

We wish to give special thanks to Sylvia Lauda for her help in developing suggested activity units and to Jean Berlfein for her help with the photography.

Barbara Blakley
Rosalie Blau
Elizabeth H. Brady
Catherine Streibert
Ann Zavitkovsky
Docia Zavitkovsky

January 1989

Contents

What is needed for school-age children?

A center which can "become the focus of social and service programs, involving families, neighbors, local businesses, civic organizations, and any other agencies in the community" with "the responsibility of serving as a bridge to the larger community in which the child lives."

From "A Statement of Principles"
Office of Child Development
Department of Health, Education, and Welfare
Washington, D.C.
1971

Introduction

This is a working notebook on planning daily activities for school-age children during the hours when they are not in the classroom and not at home. In many communities across the United States, people like you are setting up or operating child care centers where children from 5 to 10 years of age can receive the care that, for one reason or another, their families cannot give them.

The ideas and suggestions in this book have been developed by finding out what kind of care children need and what parents and guardians who place their children in centers want for them. Each program of care will be special and different in some ways, just as each child and each family the program serves will be special and different. Yet the child care centers, as well as the children and their families, will also have things in common. For instance, every child who comes to a child care program—

- needs care,   BUT needs it for a particular reason.

- spends most of his or her time at the center with children approximately the same age,   BUT at home may be an only child or one of many children.

- has a family to go home to at the end of the day,   BUT that family may be different from others in size, members, and family relationships.

- comes from a home which taught certain things and expected certain behavior,   BUT each home will have its own way and its own expectations; these may differ greatly.

- has interests, talents, habits, and values,   BUT these may be similar to those of other children in the center or they may be very different.

- will behave in certain ways learned before coming to the center,   BUT will have unique ways of behaving toward new things and people— being independent or dependent, brave or fearful, bold or shy with adults and children.

- has social and personal skills,   BUT may not have learned skills and habits others take for granted.

- has personal qualities to which others respond and personal needs which should be met,   BUT will have charm, strengths, and a special way of viewing the world that is unique to that child.

Children between the ages of 5 and 10 may come to a children's center both before school for breakfast and after school. They may be at school for three hours or more, probably five hours for the 8-, 9-, and 10-year-olds. When they come to a center, they will be looking for activities different from what has gone on in schools—just as they would if they were going home—so the pace will be different from the pace of school, more leisurely and often stretched over a longer period of time.

Elementary school-age children have developed interests and skills. They are capable of sustaining an interest in an activity if they are helped to deepen and extend their work and study. They like to attempt and to master things that are difficult. The unfamiliar is challenging, but they want to learn about it. They enjoy exploring a world which is ever-widening in both time and distance. A study of dinosaurs, for example, can entice 8-year-olds to want to build a scale model. As they research for information on what these animals ate, they begin to learn the relationship between eating habits and anatomic structures. Investigation of electronic communication from Citizen Band radios in cars and trucks to investigation of how instructions are communicated to Explorer digging on Mars could go on for months. Photography, word processors, animation, even motion pictures, are vehicles for exciting records of episodes in the children's own lives and the life of their neighborhood and school.

At this age friendships are forming. Jokes and fun with others are important. Clubs, secret passwords, and mystic signs and symbols attract. Small groups enjoy working together. There are also times when a child wants to be alone.

Children like to feel competent and be competent. The 9-year-old who says proudly that the model just completed is really *authentic* is creating standards for her own work. Children want to be expected to work carefully so they can feel pride in what they have done.

The rhythm of the program must take into account these desires to explore, to reflect, to expand, and to complete in accordance with the rhythms of individual children's tempos and interests.

Parents or guardians who choose a school-age child care program for their 5- to 10-year-olds do so for many reasons. If the staff members are to provide what the parent wants, they must understand why the child has been placed in the center and what the parent hopes for, just as they must understand what each child needs and wants.

DEVELOPMENT IN THE SCHOOL-AGE YEARS

This is a working notebook, not just a "how-to" book. It does tell you how to have fun with school-age children, those between the ages of 5 and 10, but it also tells you *why* these ways of having fun are important for the children's overall growth and development.

Those of you who already work with school-age children know how fascinating, endearing, challenging, exasperating, obnoxious, and marvelous school-age children can be—all at the same time.

Those of you who are new to this age group will find each day full of surprises—unpredictable, but never boring. You may find you prefer working with preschoolers because they are generally predictable and certainly can be counted on to be much more appreciative of you as the teacher. School-agers may appreciate you even more, but they will show it in different and sometimes hard-to-detect ways.

The ideas and suggestions in this book have been developed by finding out what kind of care children need and what parents and guardians want for them. Each program will be special and different in some ways, just as each child and family the program serves will be special and different.

You, as a teacher of school-agers, will want to make clear, when you talk to parents, that each child's needs are different. School-age boys and girls differ strikingly from their nursery school selves and how they will be later during the more often described period of adolescence. Learning to recognize these needs is particularly challenging with school-agers because, characteristically, they really don't want adults to know what is going on with them. Working with school-agers often means playing detective in order to find out what underlies an individual child's behavior.

At one time, it was thought that children between the ages of 5 and 10 went through no major changes, other than obvious but quite regular physical and mental growth. This important period was referred to as *latency,* a term from an earlier Freudian framework. Today it's clear that this view is just not accurate. The combination of our increasing knowledge of human development and the acceleration of the actual process of growing up has led to a new view of the middle years.

As those of you who are already working with school-agers are aware, increasing sex interests are a normal part of the process of development of this age group. When the older school-agers in a program show signs of preadolescence, it may be necessary to remind both yourself and the parents of your group that this is a healthy part of the growing-up process. It goes hand in hand with changes in mental capacity and social abilities. Most of all, this is a time when children are becoming increasingly aware of and responsive to influences outside their family.

This section makes no attempt to cover all available information about human development during the school years. Many readable texts provide such information, for example, *Childhood and Adolescence* by L. J. Stone and J. Church (Random House, 1973).

This section highlights *aspects* of development that those who work with school-age children need most to be aware of as they interact with children's interactions with other children.

At Seven

Central issues of development that begin around this time concern the children's perception of others, together with self-awareness and a sense of personal responsibility. Beginning around the age of 7, children become more objective about themselves and about themselves in relation to others. It is risky to link stages of growth with precise chronological ages, but, historically, age 7 has been recognized as a turning point in a child's growth, when children became pages at court or began to study for their first communion. If an extended-day program for school-agers from 5 to 10 is divided into a younger and older group, it is the second graders, the 7-year-olds, who will suddenly seem to outgrow the younger group. From one day to the next, a second grader will be ready to join the older group. Overnight, it seems, the child shows evidence of increased maturity in such areas as impulse control and personal responsibility.

Around 7 there is growth in the part of the brain associated with social skills, and there is also major intellectual growth, including the first attempts on the part of the children to avoid contradiction, especially contradiction of themselves.

Friends Count

One of the first things you notice about school-agers is how they spend as much time as possible with their friends, particularly friends of their own sex. This is especially true of the younger school-agers. As they grow older there is talk of "boyfriends" and "girlfriends" with much giggling, but there is no real dating as yet.

Instead, there is a lot of hanging around. Girls find reasons to be near a group of boys; there is much talk back and forth and some teasing. Everyone knows certain boys like certain girls and vice versa, but the romance consists of talk and often is short-lived.

Children form secret groups or clubs to keep activities secret from one another and from adults. Membership changes constantly, but is never coeducational. Typical of the school-age block structure is a sign saying "Boys keep out!" or "No girls!" Boys and girls mature at a different rate, with the girls continuing to be ahead of the boys. At this time, the whole question of masculinity and femininity becomes very important, as can be seen in the sudden, intense interest in clothes. Certain brand names of shoes and jeans are "in"; others are way, way out. There is a right and a wrong kind of hair clip and a right and a wrong kind of shoelace. There are even right and wrong colors!

Rules Count

The children have their own special culture of which clubs are just a part. A preoccupation with the rules of every game is typical of this age. During play, for example, when the rules appear to be more important than the outcome of a game, it's hard for the adult to stand by and wait to see if the children will figure out a way to resolve continuing arguments over rules themselves so the game can continue, or if adult intervention is the only way to enable the game to proceed. The children need to learn ways to solve disputes, but the rules are not always going to work in their favor. Cries of "It's not fair!" are typical of many school-age activities.

A popular game provides a good example of this process. Handball, played with a large rubber ball against a wall or backboard, gives children a wonderful opportunity to play by endless sets of rules, either with other children or by themselves. Frequently the game breaks down after disagreement over the playing rules of the moment, but then it will often resume a half-hour or so later—sometimes even sooner—and the whole process begins again. One of the children's favorite rules in handball is: After you have won a given number of points, you can make up a new rule!

Rules are all part of learning to be with and function as a member of a group, which is an important part of growing up, but it can also have its problems. Children who can't function outside a group will not learn to exercise their own judgment. Extended-day programs must make a concerted effort to encourage individuality and personal decision making, especially at this time when what peers think exerts a subtle social pressure.

The Culture

Other parts of the special school-age culture include secret passwords, mystic signs and symbols, codes, songs, and special chants, such as those used in hand-clapping games or when skipping rope. The children love word games and riddles and, in some cases, even make up languages all their own, usually adding syllables or letters to each word. Writing in code or with "invisible ink" is one of their favorite pastimes.

Collecting all kinds of things is another important part of this culture. Trading is part of collecting and lengthy negotiations are frequently in process. Just as the rules of the games change, so do the children's feelings about what is a fair trade. An exchange might be considered satisfactory to both children in the morning. By afternoon, one is complaining loudly that it wasn't fair. Bitter arguments often result. There are frequent misunderstandings and much reneging. Children will collect almost anything, but the person who invented stickers must have known something about school-agers! Collected in special books, paper stickers in all different shapes and sizes, plain, or of the "scratch 'n sniff" variety, are forever being traded. Stickers are today's equivalent of yesterday's baseball cards.

The Boys and the Girls

There is often an argumentative aspect to relations between the sexes; they will frequently make derogatory remarks about one another, but today more boys are playing hopscotch just as more girls are playing soccer and touch football. In dramatic play their games are different: Girls will play house, library, or school; boys lean toward games of haunted house or fort. But the girls can coax some of the boys into playing house with them, or (one of their favorites) to participate in mock marriage ceremonies.

There is a lot of interest in the opposite sex, particularly in terms of anatomy. Typical of this curiosity might be a child's asking where a turkey's penis is when stuffing a tom-turkey for a Thanksgiving celebration.

In spite of much progress in undoing sexual stereotyping in the nation in recent years, what is "expected" of boys and girls in this culture continues along lines that can create special emotional pressures for both. In many cases, boys are still encouraged not to cry and girls are reprimanded for showing assertive qualities. Every extended-day program can make life easier for children by challenging and discouraging sexual stereotyping. Children's self-esteem is harmed when girls are excluded from a touch football game because it's considered "too rough" for them, or when boys are ridiculed if they play with dolls or make cookies. Children need encouragement to try new games and activities on a gender-free basis.

Teachers and Parents as Models

Adult modeling both outside and inside the home is crucial at this age. The children need adults to be adults now, and, although teachers and parents can be "pals" to children, their primary role should not be overlooked or forgotten. Children suffer from anxiety at this age, as at any other. They don't need an adult expecting them to function as best friend or confidant. Turning to children for advice about adult matters gives the child too much power. It increases his anxieties and fears, which are already exaggerated at this age. Remember, fears should not be ridiculed, even though, at the moment, they may seem silly or unrealistic.

Self-Esteem

As children's self-esteem becomes more closely related to real accomplishments, there is often a lag between their own idea of what constitutes an adequate or acceptable product and what they view as "terrible" or "lousy." Some children have such unrealistically high standards for their work that they are unable to feel any satisfaction whatever from their efforts. Over and over again, paintings and drawings are ripped up and discarded. Clay is formed and re-formed. Weaving, sewing, and knitting are cast aside. What you think should be fun can be filled with difficulty and disappointment for a child. Be alert for this tendency when you are working with projects with school-agers. Don't lie to them about their work, but find a positive comment for their project.

New Ways of Thinking

In spite of the role emotions play, the children are gaining a sense of accomplishment from newly developed skills in the physical and intellectual areas. With their newfound objectivity, children are now able to see another person's point of view. They are also beginning to develop reasoning skills—the slogan of the school-ager might be said to be "It's not fair!"—and to distinguish appearance from reality. What is "real" and what *feels* real is important to the school-ager.

Logic plays a much greater role in children's thinking; the ability to do arithmetic enables the children to read and understand clocks and other aspects of time, including the "olden days"—the time when anyone over the age of 18 grew up! They are also beginning to understand maps and directions, and varying concepts of space. The development of memory and increasing language competence play an important role in the acquisition of these skills as they do in the development of conscience and moral judgment.

Ask school-agers—especially younger school-agers—what should be a logical consequence when rule such as "No hitting" is broken; the severity of their suggested consequence will be out of proportion to the seriousness of the infraction. This may be because children don't yet realize the voice of their conscience comes from inside themselves. Adult guidance can help prevent early efforts at self-government from turning into a "kangaroo court." Children will gradually understand they are their severest critic and what is meant by "let the punishment fit the crime."

School-age children are also very literal; they are unable to grasp sarcasm or irony. In any event, adults should be careful not to be sarcastic or to use ridicule in their dealings with children.

Physical Development

Children between 5 and 10 are developing many major and minor physical skills. Eye-hand coordination is improving constantly, and visual, auditory, and motor control is sufficiently developed so that most children stop reversing letters and numbers. This makes reading and spelling, as well as arithmetic, possible.

Newly developed physical skills also make school-agers better and better at sports and games. Like the preschooler, the school-ager's energy seems inexhaustible!

Finally, all this growth and change stimulates an appetite that seems impossible to satisfy. Plenty of food should be part of any school-age program. Cooking activities are wonderful ways for children to learn all sorts of concepts and skills.

***

The sections that follow outline many different kinds of activities that are appropriate for school-age children. Encourage the children to express their individuality and creativity in as many positive ways as possible, and tailor your program so that it will be responsive to each child's needs.

Daily Activities and Schedules

A good school-age child care program is a home away from home where children can play and learn. It is a safe place for parents to leave children, knowing they will be happy and well cared for. A good child care program is an extension of, not a substitute for, the home, so the program staff must see both parents and children as integral parts of the child care family.

A quality child care program is not a baby-sitting service but is planned by staff who know how children grow and develop. They are people who are interested in, and feel responsible for, seeing that the day-to-day experiences of the children take place in an environment which promotes growth and learning. Centers are usually staffed by people with special training, although some child care centers are organized and administered by parents.

A child care program for children 5 to 10 years of age serves children before and after school hours. It is also open from early morning to late afternoon during holiday and vacation periods.

The child care program staff, like the staff of any organization dealing with children, recognizes that it is an educational force. Each person on the staff serves as an example to the children, since children learn by observing as much as, if not more than, by being "taught." Parents in the home teach in this same way.

A TYPICAL DAY

During the school year, the children spend one to five hours in the center before and after school hours.

Morning: This is a time for relaxing; for cleaning up and getting ready for school; for playing a quiet indoor game or finishing homework. Someone on the staff is available for discussion, for answering questions, for helping to find materials.

Afternoon: Afternoon activities offer children longer periods of time to release pent-up energy; to work on continuing projects; to plan and go on field trips, prepare snacks, and cook new recipes; to enjoy organized sports and after-school clubs such as Brownies, Girl Scouts, Campfire Girls, and Boy Scouts. The afternoon schedule also allows time for children, with the assistance of an adult, to do their homework.

Learning to live together takes time. All groups of children will have problems, but an understanding adult can encourage and model problem-solving skills, helping children move toward the goal of resolving their own conflicts.

COORDINATING DIFFERENT SCHEDULES

Naturally there are times of the day when, because of the nature of the activity or because older children are away at school, children may be grouped together in age-similar groups. However, during the hours when the whole age span from 5- to 10-year-olds are present, age groupings should be flexible. Groupings can be by choice, by age, or by activity. Sometimes older children will help younger children; sometimes they will all participate in an activity.

Eight-, 9-, and 10-year-old children need a trusted adult close by, an adult who stays in the background but is available when needed. Children of this age are individualists who should be allowed freedom to engage in self-directed activities as long as they do not disrupt other children.

GROUP TIME

Group time is an opportunity to bring the whole group together to plan for the day, week, and year, give and receive information, discuss activity choices, share news and materials, read a story, or introduce new children.

Group time can be brief and used in a variety of ways, but it is necessary to promote a group cohesiveness.

CLEANUP

Each day during the year, housekeeping chores are done cooperatively by all the children. The center is truly a children's place, so everyone helps to clean up and keep things in order. This makes the center a homelike place and encourages children to be responsible for their environment.

SPECIAL DAYS

During vacation and holiday periods when the children are in the center all day, special planning is necessary to ensure a wide choice of activities and to include a variety of quiet/active experiences to pace the day. Rainy days, snowy days, and teacher released-time days also require special planning.

ENRICHING THE PROGRAM

The chapters that follow contain suggestions for a variety of activities. These can serve as guidelines for planning stimulating and meaningful programs with children for short or extended center hours. Lists of equipment, suggestions for storage, and a bibliography of additional readings are included.

Group times are essential in creating group cohesiveness. Children can plan, share, play a game, hear a story.

2

Figure 1.1.

School-Year Suggested Schedule

7:00–9:30 a.m.	**Center opens.** Arrival of children in accordance with parents' scheduled work hours and children's school hours. Breakfast or morning snack. Morning program adapted to interests, age levels, and hours of attendance in regular school classes.
	Indoor activities such as construction projects with blocks and accessory materials; language and literature activities with books, stories, discussion, conversation; materials such as puzzles, scissors, pegboards; card games; study area for children who want to finish their homework; records for listening; cooking.
	A brief outdoor activity period for children to stretch and release energy before returning to a quiet school-day schedule.
9:30–12:00	**Children attend** elementary classes.
12:00 noon	**Lunch** in school cafeteria or at the center for kindergarten children.
12:30–3:00 p.m.	**Kindergarten children:** Rest, washing, snack, indoor activities. Opportunities that help meet physical needs, establish routine habits, and foster positive health attitudes.
3:00 p.m.	**Group time snack,** choice of indoor or outdoor activities.
3:00–5:15 p.m.	**The teacher plans** the sequence and flow of activities to meet the needs of the children and the group's daily plan.
	Indoor activities: Blocks and accessory materials; puppets and housekeeping play; puzzles and card games; music and art materials; reading; sewing craft projects and hobbies; study; cooking; creative dramatics; creative writing; office assistance; science and nature projects; teacher-directed, small-group activity; study areas.
	Outdoor activities: Physical activities that involve running, hopping, skipping, jumping, balancing, climbing; team sports and organized games; dramatic play with boxes, ladders, boards, tarps, barrels, blocks, and other materials; gardening; woodworking; crafts projects and hobbies; science and nature projects; mud, sand, and water play; walks in the neighborhood; trips to nearby places of interest.
	Children released (according to program guidelines for release of students) to Scouts, Camp Fire Girls, Boys Club, Girls Club, YMCA, YWCA, swimming, recreation centers, dance lessons, music lessons.
5:15 p.m.	**Light snack**
5:30–6:00	**Inside and outside cleanup.** Preparation for going home and setup for the next day. Individual and small-group indoor activities. Center closes.

Figure 1.2.

Vacations and Holidays Suggested Schedule

7:00–8:30 a.m.	**Center opens.** Arrival and greeting of children in accordance with parents' scheduled work hours. Breakfast. Morning program adapted to interests, age levels, and hours of attendance. Indoor activities with blocks and similar materials; materials such as puzzles, scissors, pegboards; card games; records for listening; sewing; library corner; cooking; table games.
8:30–9:30 a.m.	**Choice of indoor/outdoor** activities, group and individual, such as puppetry, housekeeping play, music and body movement, handicrafts, cooking and baking, creative writing, drama, art, block building, construction activities, woodworking, gardening; outdoor games, soccer, play on outdoor climbing equipment, carpentry, mechanics, tetherball, roller skating, Ping-Pong™, shuffleboard.
9:30 a.m.–12:00 noon	**The teacher plans** the sequence and flow of activities to meet the needs of the children and the group's daily plan. **Snacktime.** Children help prepare and assist with snack, serving, and cleanup. **Special activity** or field trip. Group walks, swimming, day camping, water play, picnics, cycling, or teacher-directed activity.
12:00–2:00 p.m.	**Routine activities.** Washing up for lunch. Lunch. Children assist with preparation, setting tables, serving, and cleanup. Rest time according to age and needs of the children. Quiet activities such as reading, listening to records, card games, puzzles, dominoes, checkers, chess, sewing, knitting, creative writing.
2:00–5:30 p.m.	**The teacher plans** the sequence and flow of activities to meet the needs of the children and the group's daily plan. **Afternoon snack.** Children help prepare and assist with serving and cleanup. **Indoor/outdoor activities,** group and individual, should vary from those used in the morning. Children released according to release guidelines of individual program for swimming, dance lessons, music lessons, special classes, sports.
5:30–6:00 p.m.	**Inside and outside cleanup.** Preparation for going home and setup for the next day. Individual and small-group indoor activities. Center closes.

Routines: Ruts or Routes to Learning?

The daily routines of coming and going, mealtimes and snacktimes, rest, grooming, and cleanup make up the basic framework of the program in an all-day child care program. These activities can become dull and monotonous, but they need not be if a family atmosphere of helpfulness and cooperation is established.

How can this be done? First of all, it is important to find out how staff members feel about daily routines. Are they a bore? Are they chores to be completed somehow in order to get on with more important activities? Are they jobs that have to be done in a certain way, day in and day out? Or are they activities which are never done the same way twice? How can they be capitalized upon to promote children's growth and development?

When you think of the number of hours children spend every day washing, eating, resting, and cleaning up after themselves, you realize how important it is for children to enjoy routines, to learn from them and accept them as part of their everyday living. The pace for handling routines may have to be slower,

with time taken to encourage children in their first efforts. It may be necessary to become a little less or more organized than one usually is. However, it will be worth the effort if the children begin to feel that the necessary routines of life can be as interesting as other parts of the day.

ARRIVALS AND DEPARTURES: SEPARATING AND COMING TOGETHER

Hellos and goodbyes are so important. Parents as well as children need the security of knowing that someone at the center knows the child has arrived or is leaving. Greetings and goodbyes act as bridges. They help children cross over safely from home to center to school and back again. If a health check is included as part of the greeting, be sure the children know that you are interested in them, not just in their runny noses. Be sure to call

Learning to live together takes time. All groups of children will have problems, but an understanding adult can encourage everyone to learn to talk things through and get the other person's point of view.

children by name so that they know you know them; find out the name each child wants you to use.

The *way* you say "hello" or "goodbye" is even more important. Children can tell from your expression and tone of voice whether they are really welcome and whether you are sorry or glad to see them go. Arrivals and departures can be times for shared confidences—lunch box contents, dreams, TV shows, birthday presents, plans for the evening. Learn to listen to what the children are saying.

Hellos and goodbyes form the vital link between home, center, and school. They provide a chance to exchange brief reports about what the child is doing, to set dates for parent conferences, and, most of all, to let parents know you care about them and their children.

The loss of a teacher or child from the group, regardless of the reason, is another type of separation and can be upsetting to children. Recognizing this and providing opportunities for children to express their concerns validates their feelings, lowers their anxieties, and reassures them they will continue to be well cared for.

MEALTIMES AND SNACKTIMES

We can all have fun preparing and eating food together. Mealtimes in an all-day program can provide a sense of family that is so important in the lives of children. Pleasant mealtime conversations bring children and staff members in closer touch with each other; they feed children emotionally as well as physically. Mealtimes often become a time for sharing triumphs and tragedies, providing the setting for humorous or serious discussions. Children who help set the table, prepare and serve food, and clean up gain a feeling of confidence and importance in contributing to the group.

Mealtime routines can be varied frequently although family-style meals with serving dishes at the table will probably be the choice most of the time. But what could be more fun

Mealtimes and snacks can provide a sense of family that is so important in the lives of children.

than a picnic lunch on the playground, a chance for the builders to eat lunch in the block fortress they made, or breakfast in the playhouse with a best friend? Holidays and birthdays may call for special kinds of meals; children will eagerly join in the festive spirit of such occasions. For all meals, children can make the table setting attractive, help with food preparation, and have the chance to serve others, too.

Snacktimes should also be varied. Sometimes children will sit down together for a snack; at other times, children will be so involved in what they are doing that snacks can be left out on a table or "snack stand" for children to enjoy when they have time.

The chance to try a variety of foods will encourage many children to eat new things. If mealtimes are relaxed, with emphasis on consideration for others rather than formal manners, children will begin to develop good eating habits and good manners as well. Both snacks and meals can be planned with children to ensure a balanced and interesting diet. Favorite recipes can be shared with parents, who may wish to share their favorites with the center (see Chapter 13 on nutrition and cooking).

REST

The amount of rest children need will vary according to age, temperament, types of activity, weather, and energy level. Rest periods can be pleasurable—a time to sit and look at a book, to play a quiet game, to cozy into a corner with a blanket and pillow. Younger children may still want and need to sleep in a separate area; older children may enjoy resting through a low-key activity such as sewing, checkers, or reading.

A relaxed atmosphere and attitude on the part of the staff will set the stage for a relaxing rest period. Some centers have found that a brief selection of soft background music will help some children relax. Some staff members may read to a small group of children; others may go with a few children to a corner of the room for a quiet table game or a discussion. Rest period should not be so long that it becomes a battleground between staff and children. What many children need are frequent, relatively short periods of quiet time during the day.

CLEANUP

Children should be familiar with classroom routines, help the staff plan for cleanup following all activities, and check their own progress in carrying out their responsibilities. Children like having a "job board" for individual choice of a cleanup activity and individual recognition that his or her job is complete. Classroom environment, setup, and clear organization and labeling of materials assist children to become self-reliant and responsible for their own cleanup.

Sharing in cleanup jobs helps children develop a feeling of partnership with other children and the staff. Children develop a sense of pride in their part in making the center look attractive and neat.

Sometimes a child will not feel like helping or will be overwhelmed by an assigned task. Staff members can be of special help at such times, working along with the child, allowing for flexibility, and giving well-deserved recognition to the child who follows through on a difficult or disliked task. Emphasize cooperation rather than competition—except for the child's own attempts to do better each time.

GROOMING AND PERSONAL HABITS

The center can encourage good grooming and personal habits in many ways. Each child should have a special place to store an individually marked brush, comb, toothbrush, and any other items. Mirrors and facilities at child height in the bathroom will encourage attention to personal habits. While restroom facilities should always be available for children's use, additional time can be set aside before meals and after rest periods for handwashing, hair brushing, and general grooming.

The center staff can encourage a greater interest in good grooming by keeping on hand a supply of hand lotion, good smelling soap, hair clips, needles and thread. An adult giving a helping hand with a new hairdo or a compliment on a good job of hand scrubbing will encourage children to make the effort to look their best.

When they work with food, children will also have a chance to learn important health rules about clean hands and nails.

Older children might enjoy speakers and demonstrations on these subjects by people from the community such as nurses, beauticians, nutritionists.

TIPS FOR HANDLING ROUTINES

In planning for routines, here are some important points to remember:

1. Don't rush yourself or the children. Use the time spent in the activity to get to know the children better and use the learning opportunities available.

2. Enjoy the activity for its own sake. Plan the activity so that you and the children will have not only a sense of satisfaction when it is done but a sense of enjoyment while doing it.

3. Let the children do as much as possible themselves. Children can assist in planning for routines. Provide equipment that children can manage. If necessary, explain what needs to be done, then stand by to help and encourage them.

4. Vary routines as you would any other activity. Routines are the stable framework of each day, but they need not be repetitive.

5. Remember that children are learning all the time and routine times are no exception. Mathematics is used in setting tables; language skills are involved in reading and following directions; opportunities for developing good health habits come at mealtimes, rest, grooming, and cleanup times. In addition, routine activities make it possible for children to grow in self-reliance, responsibility, and cooperation.

Using Your Imagination

3

Other chapters in this book require materials like paint and clay that must be bought; this relies on ideas and scrounged materials. "Out of the mind" not "out of the store" is the theme of this chapter.

A good extended-day program encourages creativity in the children attending by making many resources readily available. School-age children are independent so materials should be out where children can reach them easily. A variety of things to stimulate the senses should be provided, including many different scrounged arts and crafts materials. Help the children use what's there, but do not present a pattern that must be followed precisely. Encourage new and different ways of creative expression and indicate your appreciation for the individual effort.

Have you ever thought of doing the same for yourself? Appreciate and encourage your own creativity. One of the challenges of working with school-agers comes from the fact that many of the children have spent several years in child care programs. Putting it succinctly, they are collaged out! As a teacher, you have exhausted the local library, or the curriculum lab of the local college, you've been through the arts and crafts books for even high school students (and these books *can* serve as a source for activities for your school-agers), and this is your third year with what may be essentially the same group of children. You're bored, and so are they. Or, you're working with children who don't seem to be interested in anything you have to offer. Perhaps they are sixth graders who need a lot of time just to hang out, listen to music, and giggle among themselves. Chances are they aren't bored, they're doing their thing. If the children are fighting a lot, however, they are bored. It doesn't pose a problem if you feel confident that there are plenty of activities and materials available, but these may have been around so long that they no longer are stimulating to the group. Activities can often be freshened by adding a few new scrounged materials (old costume jewelry for playing store, for example, or making geometric shapes out of straws and paper clips and dipping those in soapy water when the children are blowing bubbles). But sometimes new topics and approaches are required.

ACTIVITIES SCHEDULING

Take a good look at your group and make sure you are providing appropriate activities for the different times of day. Do you have a "five o'clock box" with such items as playing cards, paper games, and library books for the end of the day? Do you have enough records or cassettes with soft music for this special time? Ask parents to donate them if you do not have enough in your room. Invite the children to share their own records and cassettes. Activities should be low-key and easy to leave; at the same time you might put out games that parents would enjoy playing with their children. One such game is Mankala, an old African game also known as African chess or Pitfall in this country. It is an excellent game to have out because the kindergartners enjoy playing it just as much as fifth graders, and it lends itself to solo play as well.

Once you have made sure that you have a proper balance of activities for the different times of day, take a good look at the children in your group and observe their behavior, their interests, and their interactions. If the following are not part of your current program, you might want to consider including them.

1. *Questioning.* You can help the children develop this skill by playing games such as "20 Questions," "Who Am I?" "Hangman," and charades. Crossword puzzles and riddles also help children to develop questioning skills.

2. *Prediction.* Provide opportunities for the children to predict outcomes. Subjects can be as simple as whether it will rain tomorrow or who will win an election, or as complex as a science activity about the changing properties of household materials.

3. *Collecting.* Help the children to collect almost anything and everything within reason, and discuss how you classify different kinds of things. Help the children to set up their own systems of classification. Take time to help them share and present their collections by learning to mount or organize them in attractive ways whenever possible.

4. *Caring and teaching.* Encourage children to help one another. Comforting a younger child, teaching a game, and reading a story are all ways children can learn to care and share.

5. *Extras.* Collect and bring in such stuff as old magazines, unopened junk mail, extra calendars, wall paper, paint sample books, and rug samples. Give these to children who seem to need things of their own. Bring in broken machinery that can't be fixed; school-agers love to take apart clocks, telephones, radios, and the like.

6. *Brainstorm.* Have fun with ideas and concepts. Part of the brainstorming experience is to accept all ideas. Talk with your group, record their thoughts on big pieces of newsprint, and put them up in the room for a couple of days. You can brainstorm about almost any subject, but you might start with subjects such as eating, pets, hobbies, and different adjectives to describe a person, a tree, or a car. Think about what interests you. What would you like to learn more about? What about electricity? Do you know how motors work? Chances are if there is something you are interested in learning about, the children will be, too.

DEVELOPING THEMES

Here's an example of taking a theme from brainstorming and going with it. Take building and shelter. Children are already familiar with building through blocks, but do they know why buildings stay up? You can develop a wide variety of activities and projects around the theme of shelter, perhaps starting with caves made out of old cardboard boxes. Scrounge palm fronds in a warm climate or build an igloo in the snow where it's cold to help the children think about different ways people learned to protect themselves from the elements. (Canadian author Farley Mowatt's book *The Deer People* includes a wonderful description of how to build an igloo.) Another way to make a shelter is to use old tarps for tents and camp out for an afternoon; you

might even plan a full-scale camping trip if school schedules permit.

Planning is one key element. Making connections is another important part of this process. Stretch ideas and themes to include all aspects of the day, from snack time to quiet time model building. Here is one plan for using shelter as a theme. It is meant to serve only as an example to stimulate your own

thinking about developing new activities for your group around themes of your own. Be sure to include your children in your brainstorming; they are often your greatest resource!

EQUIPMENT

Many of these materials are listed in this category in other chapters of this book. They are grouped here to give you an example of theme planning.

Blankets
Blocks
Blueprint paper
Cardboard boxes
Carpentry tools
Chalk
Glue
Graph paper
Masking tape
Newspaper
Paper clips
Pencils
Pens
Rug samples
Rugs
Rulers
Scissors
Straws
Styrofoam pieces
Tarps
Toothpicks
Wallpaper samples
Water-based paints
Wire
Wood

MATERIALS

Books on shelter and architecture
Film strips
Films
Games such as Monopoly™, or Legos™ used to build castles
Lincoln Logs™ and other on-hand games and materials.
Old models and blueprints scrounged from an architect's office
Palm fronds
Photos
Plaster of Paris
Sand
Slides
Tree branches with leaves

STORAGE

Make sure materials are neatly stored and labeled, but also readily available. Be sure sharp tools are safely stored.

TOPICS TO TALK ABOUT WITH CHILDREN

Start with the concept of shelter, going back to its beginnings. Take a week to build a different structure every day and have snack in it. Discuss relationship of structure to environment.

Why did people come to live close to one another? The town as an adjunct to shelter.

The relationship of shelter to safety. Medieval castles and towns.

Shelter of goods. Main street versus fortress shopping centers.

Urban and suburban living—advantages and disadvantages to each.

Life on a farm. Shelter for animals.

Make up stories about your group visiting the homes of a local celebrity or a media star. You can start with the trip in a fleet of limos, and carry it right through to having the children visit the star's home and even eat a meal there before returning to the program.

IDEAS TO TRY

Build a primitive shelter such as the one with tree branches, then introduce Buckminster Fuller's dome shelter, a model of which the children can make with frozen peas and toothpicks.

Take a walk around the buildings where your program is located. Ask the custodian to show the children how the buildings are heated and cooled, where the water supply originates, and how the sprinkler system works.

Take a neighborhood walk to look at interesting houses.

Contrast buildings converted to a new use with those built for the functions they now serve.

Check local museums and art galleries for exhibits that could relate to the theme of shelter.

Have children bring in a picture of where they live or draw a picture of their home or dream house. Children could also construct shelters made of clay or wood. These can be as simple or as elaborate as children want to make them.

Invite an architect to group time and ask him or her to bring some models or plans. Visit an architect's office. Talk about what people need and want when a building is designed.

Discuss the use of color and light in building. Have children experiment with different colors and ways of light entering their structures.

Have children pair up and build structures side by side. Introduce the concept of the individual's needs and rights versus a neighbor's needs and rights. (Such an issue would be a fence that shuts out another's light).

Construct shelters for program pets, or for pets at home.

Relate the concept of shelter to transportation; construct boats with cabins, for example.

Relate shelter to weather and move to a theme on weather.

Resources

Macaulay, D. *Castle.* Boston: Houghton Mifflin, 1977.

Macaulay, D. *Pyramid.* Boston: Houghton Mifflin, 1975.

McVickar, P. *Imagination: Key to Human Potential.* Pasadena, Calif.: Pacific Oaks College, 1981.

Little, Brown publishes a series of paperback books called the *Brown Paper School Books.* A group of California teachers created the series. You will find many wonderful ideas, puzzles, problems, and activities in them.

Many communities have their own children's *Yellow Pages* and newspapers for parents. Some have special guidebooks for children.

Your local newspaper is an excellent source of information on activities for children.

Active Play and Quiet Times

4

Essential to the success of the entire program is ample, well-designed space that is adaptable to a number of uses. Both indoor and outdoor areas should be available for vigorous and creative movement activities. Care should be exercised in planning to ensure that sound levels will not interfere with other simultaneous activities of groups or individuals. Quiet space, after a busy school day, can be just as important as opportunities for expression through loud voices.

Active play in a balanced school-age program can and should include many facets. Included in such a program should be organized games where children can experience forming and working together in teams, making and following rules, and problem solving. Self-challenging activities, in which the children set goals for and compete against themselves, are especially important. Activities such as gymnastics, calisthenics, and track and field activities should be included regularly. Skills acquisition activities also play a part in a good program; children should be provided with the chance to climb, jump,

balance, swing, run, twist, and tumble, either through organized activities or through activities they have initiated and chosen themselves. Learning to make the large muscles in the body perform on command, mastering new skills, and positioning the body in space are all necessary vehicles for feelings of success and competence in every child.

Active play should also mean that children are provided with the opportunity to participate in creative movement, music, and dance. And most important, children must be allowed the opportunity to create and involve themselves in open-ended, child-centered active play in which the adult plays no specific part, and which allows the children time to run, leap, invent characters, set situations, shout, and just *be*.

A good physical development program provides children with endless opportunities for calculated risk-taking, creating self-challenging activities, and predicting and measuring successes.

Through successful participation in physical activities, children—

- develop a feeling of self-worth,
- develop courage and self-confidence to try increasingly more difficult tasks such as climbing higher and exploring new ways to perform skills,
- practice self-reliance and self-expression through creative activities such as music and dance,
- grow in ability to exercise fair play,
- have opportunities to be of service as leaders and followers through participating in games and other activities.

Wanting to touch things is perfectly natural! How much children can learn through their skin and nerves—hot and cold, soft and hard, smooth and rough. Muscles are also a source of learning—light and heavy, strong and weak.

Active physical movement is imperative for both children and adults to remain in good health. The lymph, blood, and other systems of the body function best with periods of activity ranging from exertion to quiet play.

Storage space for the equipment and materials which can enhance children's play must also be well-planned for maximum organization and protection from vandalism. Staff and children can share in the care and proper storage of these valuable additions to the program.

Safety should remain a primary consideration both indoors and out. Staff should be well-versed in first aid procedures, and first aid kits should be placed in several readily accessible areas. Local licensing regulations usually set minimum standards. Also check on insurance policies which may be necessary to protect both staff and children.

Active physical movement is imperative for both children and adults to remain in good health.

14

EQUIPMENT

Balance beam—metal or wooden, adjustable
Bars—horizontal and parallel, low for turning
Basketball goals—lower than standard
Blocks—hollow *(see Chapter 6)*
Cargo net
Cement pipes for crawling through
Climbing apparatus
Climbing pole(s)—like tetherball or higher poles
Ladder—horizontal
Mats—5′ × 10′ minimum, for tumbling
Piano and other musical instruments
Poles or logs embedded in earth
Record player and records
Rings—safely mounted at various heights
Ropes—two, about two feet apart, for swinging between trees
Sandbox
Tetherball equipment
Tires—for climbing through or as swings
Walls for hitting balls against

MATERIALS

Balloons
Balls—soft plastic fleece balls; crocheted balls stuffed with old stockings; rubber balls, 6″, 8″, 13″; utility ball, 8½″; softball; and basketball
Barrel—55 gallon steel drum to crawl through
Bats—unbreakable plastic and/or wood
Beanbags
Cones—for hurdles or goals
Frisbees
Hoops—can be made from ½″ polyethylene hose or ⅝″ doweling, glue, and electrician's tape
Inner tube—cut in pieces for pulling
Inner tubes—inflated

Jump rope—#12 sash cord, nylon or plastic
Jumping boards
Mirror
Nets
Paddles—wooden or made from metal clothes-hanger covered with silk or nylon
Parachute—16′, from surplus stores
Pump—for air for balls
Rings—deck tennis (rubber)
Sawhorses
Scarves and props for dancing
Stilts—made with cord and cans or purchased wood or aluminum
Stopwatch
Wands—36″ batons or dowels
Yo-yos

SPECIALLY MARKED OUTDOOR AREAS

Squares for four-square game
Number and letter squares
Hopscotch
Shuffleboard
Basketball
Volleyball
Tetherball
Wheel toy paths
Skating and biking areas

STORAGE

Bicycle racks
Dowel pegs or hooks—for hanging hoops, jump ropes
Padlock and chain—for securing items such as tires to fence
Pegboard—attached to wall, marked for hanging small items
Sandbox cover
Shelves

TOPICS TO TALK ABOUT WITH CHILDREN

Care and storage of equipment.

Forming of teams—assessing strengths and weaknesses.

Individual assessment—methods for measuring individual progress in skill-building activities.

Different methods of building particular skills.

Combining skills and materials for creative dance.

Developing awareness of movement and growth.

Need for consistent rules for participation in organized activities.

Safety rules for use of special equipment.

Roles of supervisory adults.

IDEAS TO TRY

(You should adapt these ideas to the ages and abilities of your children.)

Arrange tournaments or decathlons for mastering particular skills.

Children can prepare individualized charts to measure their progress in certain activities.

Children can use a stopwatch to measure and record their progress in self-challenging activities. Stress that children are only in competition with themselves.

Form teams and elect team captains for sports such as softball (or tee-ball for younger children), volleyball, badminton, and soccer.

Children can create an obstacle course using barrels, tires, inner tubes, tumbling mats, and other equipment.

Children can invent relay games.

Creative movement activities can involve props (scarves, capes, hats, umbrellas, crepe paper) and music selected by the participants.

Study different ethnic folk dances; design and make authentic apparel.

Arrange for "activity days" (bike day, skating day, gymnastics day) when children bring their equipment from home.

Plan a "Junior Olympics" activity involving children from a neighboring school or center.

Maintain an equipment storage area available on a daily basis for children's selections.

Encourage the use of special accessories to enhance movement experiences (balloons for balancing games and relays, blindfolds for sensory experiences, etc.).

Children can create their own climbing and/or balancing structures by collecting plastic milk storage boxes.

Create an interest center within the classroom using exercise ropes, tumbling mat, bean-bag toss, etc.

A record player, an assortment of records, and instruments can be available at all times for spontaneous music or dance activities—ask children to bring their favorite records.

Resources

Arnold, A. *The World Book of Children's Games.* New York: Fawcett World Publishing, 1975.

Bartal, L., and Ne'eman, V. *Movement Awareness and Creativity.* New York: Harper & Row, 1975.

Corbin, C.B. *Inexpensive Equipment for Games, Play, and Physical Activities.* Dubuque, Iowa: William C. Brown, 1972.

International Council on Health, Physical Education, and Recreation. *ICHPER Book of Worldwide Games and Dances.* Washington, D.C.: American Association for Health, Physical Education, and Recreation, 1967.

Millen, N. *Children's Games from Many Lands.* New York: Friendship Press, 1965.

Sullivan, M. *Feeling Strong, Feeling Free: Movement Exploration for Young Children.* Washington, D.C.: National Association for the Education of Young Children, 1982.

Werner, P.H., and Simmons, R.A. *Inexpensive Physical Equipment for Children.* Minneapolis, Minn.: Burgess, 1976.

Arts and Crafts

5

Using real tools and materials, children can create things they feel proud of and which others will enjoy and admire. Children can work with art materials alone (even in a room full of other people), or they can enjoy the company of special friends. By capturing moments of their lives in a variety of shapes, forms, and colors, children can continue to enjoy these reminders of people they know and places they have been.

With art children can describe their feelings, experiences, wishes, and ideas in ways that have meaning for them and are understandable to others. Through pounding clay, covering a sheet of paper with dark colors, or meaningless repetition of drawings, children can also express feelings—feelings they may not be able to express in words.

Painting or drawing with bright or gloomy colors, slicking and smoothing a clay fish with water, using soft cotton for clouds, making rough scratchy lines with an almost dry brush, children can learn how color, shape, size, and texture make the finished product look the way it does. As they choose and combine

17

objects of different colors, shapes, and textures, children learn to become more careful observers of the materials they are using and of the world around them.

Arts and crafts projects can teach children new ways of creating with ordinary things: making mobiles and wire sculptures from coathangers; using clay for beads, pendants, and plaques, as well as for bowls and figures; painting on cardboard, wood, and foil, as well as paper. Such projects can stimulate children to think up their own ways of using almost anything to create something new.

Cutting and twisting wires, rolling clay, balancing the delicate parts of a mobile, lifting and carrying, all help children learn to work with their large and small muscles and develop hand-eye coordination. Opportunities

to cut metal with tin snips, punch holes in leather with an awl, saw on a curved line with a coping saw, glaze and fire special clay products, take and develop photographs, help children learn to use a variety of tools and equipment skillfully and safely. Choosing a project, listening to or reading directions, planning, making a decision as to what tools and supplies to use, sticking with the project over a period of time, solving problems, working together or asking for help, all of these help children develop effective work habits. Children also learn that cleaning up and returning materials and equipment to their storage place is important if these things are to be found the next time they are needed.

Big projects such as painting and decorating a puppet stage or composing a mural, or small projects done at the same table or in the same area, can help children learn to work together —to take turns, share, give and accept help, and value and protect other children's work. Through such projects children have opportunities to find out that not everyone likes the same things and that this is alright.

Working together or alone, children hear and learn to use new words to describe their tools, materials, and processes involved in their projects. They have many opportunities to find out and talk about one another's plans, ideas, needs, and feelings. Reading directions and labels on supplies and shelves and using books about how our ancestors worked with arts and crafts help children enrich their vo-

Arts and crafts projects can teach children new ways of creating with ordinary things — using clay for beads.

cabularies and understand how reading can be both useful and interesting.

Meaningful art experiences can promote a growing awareness of aesthetics—developing an appreciation for beauty through balance, form, line, and color. Individuals can evaluate their skills and selection of materials as they mature in their understanding of the many facets of art exploration. Comparing and contrasting various cultural art forms and expressions can lead to new insights about the universality of expression through art.

Children can coordinate their experiences in a variety of other activities through art— writing and illustrating a book detailing the emergence of a butterfly or creating stage sets for an original musical production. Many projects can take on new dimensions when they are taken outdoors to a table or a grassy spot under a cool tree. Whatever its form, art can enhance children's understandings of themselves and the world around them.

EQUIPMENT

Air sprayer
Aprons
Brayer
Brushes—various sizes, types, and shapes
Camera
Clay boards
Crochet hooks
Darkroom equipment
Drip cloths
Drying rack, shelves
Easels, bulletin boards, display screens
Hole punches
Labels

Linoleum tools and blocks
Looms
Matting knife
Measuring tapes
Modeling and stamping tools for leather
Mounting pins
Needles—knitting, sewing; varied sizes
Paper cutter
Plastic bottles, tubs
Rags and towels for cleanup
Rubber bands
Rulers
Scissors—right- and left-handed styles, assorted
  sizes
Sewing machine
Sponges
Stamp pads
Staplers
Thumb tacks

MATERIALS

Absorbent cotton
Beads, feathers, sequins
Cardboard—various weights and sizes
Chalk—assorted colors
Charcoal
Clay—commercial
Cloth—various widths, colors, textures, designs
Copper
Cords
Cottage cheese cartons and lids
Crayons
Dyes of various colors, types
Enamel paints
Felt
Felt pens
Film
Finger paints
Foil, aluminum
Gummed tape—assorted widths
Liquid soap
Mesh screening

Metallic thread
Modeling media—flour and salt, plasticine,
  sawdust
Natural items—acorns, seeds, grasses, flowers,
  cones, stones, pebbles, corn shucks, leaves,
  nutshells
Paper—crepe, gummed, tissue, construction,
  butcher, parchment, easel, newsprint, white
  drawing, waxed, roll for murals, old telephone
  books, wallpaper books
Paper bags, plates, boxes, picture files
Paste, glue, rubber cement
Pencils
Pictures—postcards, old Christmas cards
Pins
Pipe cleaners
Plaster of Paris
Plastic—assorted sizes and shapes
Plastic paint
Potato mashers
Reed raffia
Ribbons, rickrack, edging
Sand
Sawdust
Scotch tape
Shellac
Soap bars for sculpting
Soap flakes

Spools—wood and plastic
Starch
Styrofoam—various shapes and sizes
Tempera paints
Thread—sewing, embroidery
Tiles—wall board
Trays
Turpentine
Vegetable colors
Water colors
Water soluble inks
Wax
Wax paper
Wire
Wire coathangers
Yardage
Yarns

STORAGE

Boxes, baskets, barrels, and shelves for organized storage
Labels for storage units—store items together
  in one place
Shelves of different heights and widths
Racks or hooks for aprons—near area where
  they will be used

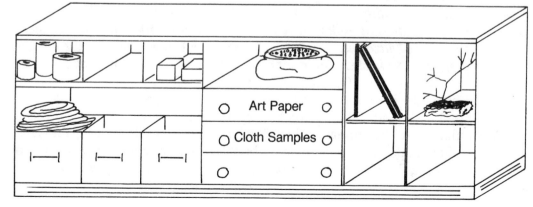

Storage Unit

19

TOPICS TO TALK ABOUT WITH CHILDREN

Care and safe use of tools, preparation of materials and equipment.

Steps to be considered and materials needed for projects—children may wish to list what they will be doing.

Materials can be brought from home—empty spools, egg cartons, plastic containers, etc.

Creative use of odds and ends for collages.

Children may want to plan for an art show of their projects—another center or school could be invited, as well as parents.

What happens to paint when water, starch, soap, or sand is added?

Discovering new ways to use familiar materials—tempera paint, finger paint, water paint, colors, charcoal, colored chalk, clay, dough clay, crayons, felt pens, soap.

Ways older children can work with younger children to complete a difficult project.

How to make mats and picture frames.

New words—*titanium white, ivory black, cadmium orange, cadmium yellow light, phthalocyanine blue, alizarine, crimson, ochre, burnt sienna.* New ideas for some children—hot and cold colors (red, orange, and yellow; blue, green, and purple); primary colors (red, yellow, and blue); secondary colors (mixtures of two primary colors—red and yellow make orange; blue and yellow make green; blue and red make purple).

Children may wish to make plans for trips to art exhibits and museums and to explore the neighborhood. What arrangements need to be made?

Who might children know—a grandparent, neighbor, sister, or brother—who can teach children a new skill or technique or discuss art objects from another culture?

IDEAS TO TRY

Clay and other modeling media

Commercial clay (gray or terra-cotta). Wet commercial clay is easiest to use, although it is also available in powdered form. Wet clay must be kept in an airtight container, such as a plastic bag, with a wet sponge to keep it damp and ready for use.

String or wire can be used to cut lumps at least the size of a grapefruit for each child. A hard surface such as a board or linoleum block makes work with clay and cleanup easier. Any clay temporarily not being worked with should be covered with a damp cloth until the entire project is finished. Few tools are needed for work with clay—designs may be scratched in with fingernails or other objects; textured items can be added or used to vary the surface. Children may wish to explore several types of construction: slab, pinch, coiling, draping.

If a kiln is available for firing the clay, all air bubbles must be removed from the object. Check on details before undertaking projects of this magnitude.

Plasticine. Plasticine is readily available, but children may prefer more natural clays or modeling media which can be mixed easily and inexpensively in the classroom.

Dough clays. Several recipes are available for variety in texture, ease of storage, and possibilities for reuse. Experiment to find the children's favorite types.

Flour and salt clay	
4 cups flour	Food coloring
1 cup salt	Water to moisten
Mix the ingredients to desired dampness. Store in refrigerator to avoid spoiling. This clay dries hard and can be painted or decorated with pens.	
To make reusable dough, add two tablespoons of cooking oil.	

Sawdust modeling	
2 cups sawdust	1 cup flour or wheat paste
Liquid starch	1 tablespoon glue (if flour is used)
Mix to workable consistency. Can be dried and painted.	

Collage

A base of a paper plate, shirt cardboard, construction paper, wood, wall board, boxes, or any surface which will hold a variety of materials can be used. Glue may be needed as a better adhesive than paste for heavier items. Children should be encouraged to consider size, shape, color, and variety. Lace, flowers,

Working with clay helps children learn to use their large and small muscles and develop hand-eye coordination.

Construction

Three-dimensional constructions can be made with one or many materials, and they can be representational or abstract. Constructions which remain fixed are called stabiles; those which are made to move are called mobiles.

Children will need to consider how things will be attached so they will hold together in a three-dimensional design. Wood, tongue depressors, swab sticks, wire, coathangers, wood pieces, aluminum foil, thread, corrugated cardboard may be used. Many interesting arrangements can be made by using cellophane, thin colored plastics, jewelry, colored sticks, colored string, and yarn. Cardboard tubes, pipe cleaners, pieces of wood, small wooden dowels, construction paper, and cardboard cylinders can be used for wood gluing.

Essential tools needed are scissors, cutting pliers, hammer, hole punch, and stapler. Thread, wire, string, yarn, or fine chain can be used for hanging mobiles, but bases are needed for stabiles. Stabiles and mobiles provide wonderful opportunities for creative expression—line, form, shapes, colors, textures, balance, and manipulation.

Toothpick, tongue depressor, straw, or string constructions can be made with paste or glue, scissors, and tissue paper. Toothpicks may be glued to a bent reed, pushed into a styrofoam base, or glued on wire. String constructions may be made on a notched cardboard or wood base with tubes and small boxes.

shells, velvet, netting, satin, styrofoam, pipe cleaners, paper lace doilies, pieces of cork, yarn, and buttons are just some of the materials that can be used. If at all possible, use nonfood items for all craft uses—other materials have more satisfactory qualities.

Wax collage is a variety children may wish to try if adequate safety precautions are taken. Materials and equipment you will need are: hot plate, double boiler, wax, collage materials, and cardboard. Melt wax in pan. Children then carefully pour a small amount of wax on cardboard to create a design and decorate hot wax with collage materials.

21

Toothpick Sculpture

Wire sculpture can be created from wire bent to form shapes and designs, curled around pencils, tubes, spools, or boxes. Stovepipe wire will retain shape. Scissors and pliers are needed. Mount on base if desired.

Bookends can be made from small boxes which are decorated and then filled with sand.

A delightful **wall hanging** can be made quickly from cloth such as felt or burlap, crayons, doweling, string, blunt needle for tapestry work, yarn or embroidery thread.

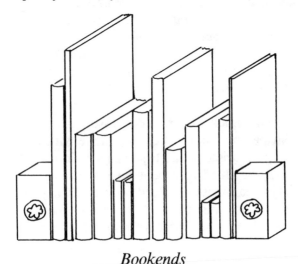

Bookends

Designs with crayons can be ironed with two pieces of paper folded around the fabric to absorb the wax. Yarn or thread can be used to sew the heading before inserting the dowel; the string is used for hanging the tapestry.

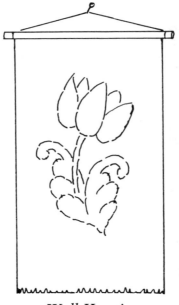

Wall Hanging

Aluminum foil will twist, bend, and squeeze into various shapes and designs. Fast drying cement may be used to join pieces together only when children are old enough to understand the extreme care needed to use the glue. Embellishments may be old jewelry, feathers, beads, enamel paints, ribbons.

Decorate jewelry boxes, wastepaper baskets, desk blotter sets, instruments, tote bags, knitting and sewing boxes.

Make animals, people, hats, transportation toys, miniature doll furniture, houses, pet cages, trays, sorting boxes, puppet theaters, shoeshine kits.

Crayons, colored chalk, charcoal, inks, felt pens, and pencils

Crayons can be used on the side if the paper covering is removed. Colors will be bright if there is a cushion of newspapers or magazines under the drawing paper. A pleated fold of construction paper or light cardboard makes a good holder for crayons, chalk, and charcoal.

Use pieces of torn cardboard or paper as a **stencil**—rub colored chalk or crayons along the edges of the stencil, put it on the paper and then brush the chalk off the stencil onto the paper with tissue. A pencil eraser can be used to rub the crayon onto the paper if a hard wax crayon is used. Nonaerosol hair spray or fixative should be used over chalk or charcoal work.

Crayon rubbings can be done on any thin paper over stones, leaves, cardboard pieces of various thicknesses and shapes, sandpaper, or corrugated paper.

To make a **crayon resist or etching,** cover white paper with crayons (use one or more crayons), then, using a black crayon, cover the entire paper. Use a blunt needle, nail, edge of scissors, or comb and scratch until design and colors show through. Thin paint (with a little liquid soap added) can also be used to cover the design.

Chalk painting can be done with the addition of starch on any kind of wet paper or cardboard. The end of the piece of chalk can be sharpened for fine work or blunted for thick lines. Use a tissue, rag, or fingers to mute and brush the colors.

Colored chalk soaked in a strong sugar-water solution for ten minutes will smear less while in use. A fixative for spraying colored chalk artwork may be made by dissolving gum arabic in water until it is the consistency of cream. Use an empty spray bottle as container and spray.

Charcoal work can be done the same as chalk painting.

Melted crayons are a good way to use up small pieces. Cut or scrape pieces of crayon onto shiny shelf paper or finger paint paper and put this between two pieces of waxed paper. Cover with newspaper and press with warm iron to melt and spread the crayons.

For a variation, use two pieces of paper. Remove the top one after melting the crayons and scratch a design into the soft wax. Children can also put crayon pieces into bags and smash with a mallet. Bits of crayon are then sprinkled on paper and set out in the hot sun to melt.

Inks may be used on wet paper, as water colors or finger paints. Inks can also be used over crayon work.

Felt pens can be used singly or in combination with many other arts and crafts activities.

Pencils, lead of varied colors and degrees of hardness and softness, are vital for drawing activities. They can be combined with other media or used with graph paper for sketching and planning.

Scribble-Scrabbles

Construction paper
Pencils with thick, dark lead
Felt pens, crayons, waterproof ink and pen, or tempera paint and brush

Scribble design over entire paper in one continuous and abstract line. Outline portions of the pattern or design with felt pen, ink, or paint.

Old Masters Printing

Typing paper, white or colors—2 pieces	Wax crayons
Piece of window screen the size of the paper	Cloth or paper towels
Can of turpentine or mineral spirits	Cardboard or newspapers

Cover table with cardboard or newspapers. Draw design on paper placed over the screen, pressing heavily with the crayons. Lift picture off and spread back of paper with a thin coat of turpentine or mineral spirits; this will soften the wax crayon. Place another piece of paper over the drawing and rub with fingers until the picture is transferred as a monoprint. It may be possible to take two or three monoprints from the same drawing, as in finger painting.

Finger Painting

Finger painting can be done indoors or out on a variety of surfaces and in a number of ways. Experiment with different techniques and recipes. A few drops of oil of clove prevents distressing odors. Be sure to keep mixtures in covered jars in a cool location.

Finger Paint Mixture #1

1 cup liquid starch	6 cups warm water
½ cup soap chips	Dry tempera or food coloring

Dissolve soap chips with enough water and stir until all lumps have disappeared. Add to starch and remaining water. Keep in covered plastic jar until ready to use. Color may be added as children paint or in the mix.

Finger Paint Mixture #2

½ cup cornstarch	2 teaspoons glycerine
1⅓ cups boiling water	Dry tempera or food coloring
½ cup soap flakes	

Dissolve cornstarch in boiling water until it is a cold cream consistency. Add soap flakes and glycerine and keep in covered jar. Color may be added to the mixture at this time or as the children paint.

Finger Paint Mixture #3

1½ cups laundry starch	1 quart boiling water
1½ cups soap flakes	Tempera paint (dry or liquid)
½ cup talcum powder (optional)	

Dissolve starch with some cold water until it is a cold cream consistency. Add the boiling water and cook until the finger paint mixture looks somewhat transparent. Keep stirring and add the talcum powder. Cook before adding the soap flakes, stirring until they are evenly distributed. Store in covered jars. Color may be added before placing in jar or when children are ready for work.

Finger Paint Mixture #4

Liquid starch   Dry tempera or food
½ cup soap   coloring
    chips (optional)

Leave bottle of starch open for two or three days for the mixture to thicken, or add ½ cup of soap chips. Add color when ready to use finger paint.

Finger Paint Mixture #5

1 cup cornstarch   4 cups boiling water
2 cups cold water   1 cup soap flakes
2 envelopes plain   Dry tempera
    unflavored gelatin

Dissolve cornstarch in 1½ cups of cold water. Soak gelatin in remaining ½ cup of cold water. Add starch mixture to hot water slowly. Cook over medium heat, stirring constantly until mixture is thick and glossy. Blend in gelatin and soap flakes until dissolved. Divide into portions as desired and add tempera. Keep in covered jar.

Finger Paint Mixture #6

Wallpaper paste   Tempera paint
    (wheat paste)   Lukewarm water

Mix wallpaper paste into lukewarm water and stir until smooth. Add tempera paint. Measure your first try of this recipe and add either paste or water until you have the consistency you wish, then write the recipe for your file.

Monoprint from Finger Painting

Finger Paint
Oilcloth taped to table or formica-covered
    tabletop
Waxed shelf paper or finger paint paper

Finger paint directly on the oilcloth or table surface. Press the waxed shelf paper or finger paint paper on top of the wet painting and smooth over entire surface with palm of hand until the painting is transferred to the paper. It may be possible to take two or three prints from the same finger painting. When dry, place painting face down between two pieces of newspaper and iron.

Jewelry

Beads from Flour and Salt

2 cups flour
2 cups salt
2 tablespoons powdered alum
Dry tempera or food coloring
Water
Toothpicks or nails
Rolling pin
String, narrow strips of leather, yarn, ribbon, or
    plastic lacing
Large ball of clay
Shellac
Brush (narrow bristles)
Alcohol for cleaning brush

Mix alum, flour, salt, water, and coloring until consistency of putty. It is now ready to be made into beads in a variety of ways:

- Make long coil and cut into pieces.
- Roll a piece between palms.
- Flatten out with rolling pin as if making dough ready for cookie cutter.

Using either a toothpick or nail, punch hole through each of the beads. Insert the toothpick or nail into hole and stick it into clay ball. Turn the nail or toothpick around in the beads from time to time to keep them from drying in the bead. Shellac beads when dry and then dry again.

Sizes and shapes may be irregular, and small beads can be placed between larger beads for design purposes. String may also be knotted between beads.

Finger painting and many other art projects can be done indoors or out.

Leather

Leather scraps and pieces can be purchased. Needed are modeling and stamping tools, hole puncher, lacing, scissors, and a wooden mallet. Leather can be used on collages, glued onto wood as bookends, and made into billfolds, key rings, and other objects. Wet leather with sponge and press down with the modeler to bring desired design into relief.

Nature Crafts*

When working with natural objects, make certain conservation measures are followed to preserve living plants and animals.

You may wish to press and make leaf prints through spatter painting. Seeds can be used to make natural dyes and paints. Driftwood can serve as the base for stabiles.

Painting

Easel paint with tempera paints on cardboard, cloth, wood, construction paper. Paint indoors or out at tables, on floor, on boards attached to fences.

Spray paint (nonaerosol) boxes, boards, carpentry pieces, clay beads, pine cones.

Enamel paint on cardboard, wood, toys, furniture, clay beads. Always use unleaded paint.

Water paint on sidewalks and buildings, outside equipment, and on paper.

Paint on **clay** ready for kiln or dried clay objects.

*See Chapter 14 on science.

Paint with **rollers;** use rollers with string or cord on base to create design.

Print with paints; use found objects and gadgets.

Textile paint to create wall hangings, place mats, fabric for sewing.

Blow through **straws** to create unique designs, blend colors.

Develop **new techniques;** encourage children to combine two or more ideas. Experiment with various shapes, sizes, and kinds of paper. What happens when the paper is wet or dry?

Painting with Colored Ink on Cloth

White blotter
Masonite™; smooth, flat board; or heavy cardboard
Cloth of thin linen, rayon, or unbleached muslin
Waterproof ink
Fine point brush or lettering pen
Pencil

Place blotter on board. Pencil design on blotter, making sure that all lines are heavy. Cut cloth large enough to cover the design and place over blotter so design shows through. Use ink sparingly—blotter will absorb surplus (large areas in the design should be covered with small strokes instead of water color wash techniques.)

Sand Painting

Combine ¼ part tempera powder to 1 part sand; mix and put in large shakers. Shake sand mixture on paper children have covered with paste.

String Painting

Block of wood
Glue
Thick string
Cloth or paper
Tempera paint or water-soluble block-printing ink

Place several thicknesses of newspaper on table. Place glue in flat container, rub block of wood into the glue on one side. Turn block over and design the string on the glue side; leave until dry. Press design block into ink or paint and print on cloth or paper. Overprints may be made by using other blocks and designs and different color paints or inks.

Blocks can be used to make several copies, dried to use again, or string can be pulled off and another design placed on fresh glue.

Ink Painting

Paper
Water colors and brushes
Artist ink pens and ink

Children wash surface of paper with water colors or plain water, then use pen and ink to draw a design on the wet surface.

Paste

1 cup flour
1 tbsp powdered alum
1 to 1½ pints hot water
several drops of oil of cloves

Mix alum and flour in cold water until a smooth mixture. Add the boiling water and cook for 2 to 3 minutes. Add the drops of oil of cloves.

Paper

All sizes, shapes, colors, textures may be used for tearing, folding, twisting, curling, bending. Paper may be fringed, braided, scored, wrinkled, slit, bunched up, or used to weave. Crepe paper can be pulled through a hole, stretched, and used as yarn. Because paper is a natural resource, it should never be wasted.

Papier-mâché can be used for masks, jewelry, puppets, marionettes, toys, and as a base for other art media. Quick papier-mâché can be made from rolled up or folded newspapers. String is used to tie material into desired shapes that are then covered with wheat paste to which tempera coloring has been added. When almost dry, the rolls can be shaped into designs, then dried. Sometimes stapled pieces can help hold the total project together. Papier-mâché can be added around empty plastic bottles to give shape and design, then painted and shellacked.

To make papier-mâché, tear newspapers into narrow strips, about ½-inch wide, and pull them through a shallow dish containing a creamy mixture of wallpaper (wheat) paste and water. Coat the paper with the paste, and wipe off the excess with your fingers. Carefully wrap the strips around a bottle or bucket or other object. Apply approximately three layers of paper, each layer in a different direction for added strength. Be certain to smooth all cracks and loose edges on the final paper coat. Allow the paper to dry thoroughly for several days, then remove the supporting object. After the paste is dry, cover the papier-mâché with a single coat of white paint, thinned plaster, or regular white acrylic-based wall paint. Then paint designs and finish with a spray (nonaerosol) plastic, shellac, or varnish coat.

Mosaics may be made with colored pieces of paper instead of tiles.

For **strip paper sculpture,** cut paper into various widths. Bend into forms and join by staples, paste, or paper fasteners.

Newspapers can be twisted into shapes after a thin paste has been spread over them. Dry, then paint with tempera or add yarn, buttons, beads, feathers, toothpicks, etc.

Paper plates can serve as a base for masks, collages, puppets, tambourines, clocks, wall plaques, stitching designs, note holders, etc.

Sculpture

For **plaster of Paris sculpture,** mix 4 cups plaster of Paris with 1 quart of water. Pour into milk carton or similar container until dry and hard. Older children can remove and carve with a knife into desired design.

Soap may be used to sculpt a design and/or used as a base for sequins, beads, jewelry designs.

Sticks may be glued together to form a design. They may be constructed erect or flat on the table so pieces may be added while the project is drying.

Trips

Where can you accompany children so that they can see how art serves esthetic purposes and is used as a practical part of life? Try art galleries; art supply stores; art shows; nature walks; libraries for art and architecture books;

bookstores to see prints; fabric stores to notice designs; gardens, backyards, or farmers markets to see fruits and vegetables; markets to look at designs; jewelry stores; pottery shops; puppet and marionette shows; print shops; hobby shops; and many other places where children can see art, experience it, and learn from it.

Resources

Bos, B. *Don't Move the Muffin Tins.* Roseville, Calif.: Turn-the-Page Press, 1978.

Brittain, W.L. *Creativity, Art and the Young Child.* New York: Macmillan, 1979.

Cardozo, P., and Menten, T. *The Whole Kids Catalog.* New York: Bantam, 1975.

Cobb, V. *Arts and Crafts You Can Eat.* Philadelphia: J.B. Lippincott, 1974.

Fiarotta, P. *Snips and Snails and Walnut Whales.* New York: Workman, 1975.

Guth, P. *Crafts for Kids.* Blue Ridge Summit, Pa.: TAB Books, 1975.

Hardiman, G.W., and Zernick, T. *Art Activities for Children.* Englewood Cliffs, New Jersey: Prentice-Hall, 1981.

Jenkins, P.D. *Art for the Fun of It.* Englewood Cliffs, New Jersey: Prentice-Hall, 1980.

Lasky, L., and Mukerji, R. *Art: Basic for Young Children.* Washington, D.C.: National Association for the Education of Young Children, 1980.

Newmann, D. *The Early Childhood Teacher's Almanac Activities for Every Month of the Year.* West Nyack, New York: Center for Applied Research in Education, 1984.

Sattler, H.R. *Recipes for Art and Craft Materials.* New York: Lothrop, Lee & Shepard, 1973.

Zarchy, H. *Papercraft.* New York: World Publishing Co., 1966.

Construction helps children learn how to size up problems and to figure out ways of dealing with the problem.

28

Blocks

6

Whether indoor or outdoor, blocks give children of all ages opportunities to become masters of space and materials as they build towers of hollow blocks, bridges with arches and columns that span the room, or tiny structures with small table blocks, big enough for only one doll or matchbox car. There are opportunities to create: roads for cars to travel on, hideouts or clubhouses to escape to, buildings to play house in, cages to contain scary monsters, rockets and spaceships for trips to outer space, and castles to live in. Children can be caught up in the beauty of shape, balance, and color as they constantly change what they are building and add decorations. There are times when everybody wants to help with the project; this creates opportunities for the children to share feelings of satisfaction, achievement, and cooperation.

While it is fun to see the finished product, there is just as much pleasure in the process of creating it. Tearing a structure down and starting over again is very much a part of this, for although blocks themselves are solid, they are as flexible in use as the child's imagination. There is no one way to use blocks; children of all ages may work near each other. A mighty fortress may rise right beside a flat, row-of-blocks road.

By lifting, carrying, bending, reaching, grasping, holding, and pushing blocks of all kinds, children have opportunities to develop large and small muscles, and muscular coordination. At the same time, delicately adding one more block to a tower, sliding a car in and out of an archway, or getting more blocks without bumping into everything, helps children sharpen hand-eye coordination.

Children can learn new words by using and naming ramps, pillars, arches, cylinders, and cubes. They can also learn to tell other children their ideas, needs, and wishes — "That's mine," "I'll trade you things," "If you put that there, it will fall down." As they play with blocks, children can learn a great deal about getting along with others of all ages — such as respecting the ideas and property of others, waiting for and taking turns, sharing, and compromising. Construction helps children learn how to size up problems — for example, that the roof planks are too short for the building — and to figure out ways of dealing with the problem — using different roofing materials, moving the walls closer together, eliminating the roof. With blocks, children have wonderful opportunities for make-believe as they change and extend their dramatic play and for converting the vast world around them into a smaller, more manageable one by building and using approximations of the objects in that world: roads, stores, train stations, bridges, walls, space modules. Using the many different kinds of blocks, accessories, and surroundings that are part of this kind of play, children can begin to understand such abstractions as:

Shape — by using rectangular, triangular, cylindrical, and cone-shaped blocks and large and small cubes.

Space — by making buildings big enough to get into, or by building in large yards or in smaller rooms among other children.

Height — by building flat roads, ranch houses, skyscrapers, or forts.

Similarities and differences — by looking for a certain kind of block to plug a hole in an almost-finished wall, or by sorting blocks and putting them back where they belong.

Numbers and mathematical relationships — by counting blocks, placing two half-size blocks together to make a whole block, placing two blocks together to make a double block, or even by feeling that there are "too many" to pick up alone at cleanup time.

Safety—by building out of the way of doors and places where people walk, lining up corners for sturdiness, and staying within certain limits. But the limits should be based on the kind of space, number and ages of the children, and what they have already demonstrated they can handle. Limits should never be arbitrary.

Children benefit from opportunities to wonder, experiment, discover, master materials, and assume responsibilities when they build with blocks.

EQUIPMENT

We recommend the following as a minimum for groups of 15 children.

FLOOR BLOCKS—approximately 480 pieces
  28 pillars
  28 half-units
  192 units
  100 double units
    48 quadruple units
    20 roofing boards
    20 ramps
    12 triangles
     8 arches
     8 quarter-circle arches
     2 half-circle arches
     1 Y switch
     1 X switch
    12 large cylinders

HOLLOW BLOCKS
  12 units
  18 double units

    6 quadruple units
    6 cleated boards
   12 plain boards

PARQUETRY BLOCKS

WOOD-SNAP BLOCKS

TABLE BLOCKS—design blocks, plastic blocks, open-sided blocks

ADDITION CUBES, DOMINOES

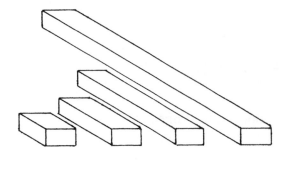
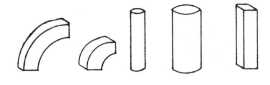
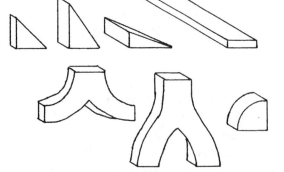

Floor Blocks

ACCESSORY MATERIALS

TRANSPORTATION AND DRAMATIC PLAY—sturdy plastic and wooden cars, carts, steering wheels, delivery trucks, school buses, firetrucks, boats, jeeps, planes, helicopters, trains, freight, passengers, wheelbarrows, tricycles, wagons, derricks, roadmaking equipment, bell for train, megaphone, play money, engineer's hats, paper for tickets, discarded license plates, cash register boxes, ladders, heavy cardboard for roofs, telephones, dashboard, boards for counters in train stations, traffic signs.

PEOPLE AND ANIMALS—plastic or rubber community people of various ages, ethnic groups, and occupations; domestic animals.

PICTURES AND PHOTOGRAPHS—buildings, cities, maps, dams, streets, urban and rural scenes, architecture of different countries, airports, docks.

MISCELLANEOUS—rugs, blankets, tarpaulin, clothespins, telephone wire, string, pieces of rubber tubes, spools, cans, cones, wheels, old radios, empty food cartons, paper boxes, hats and clothing, gas and air pumps, fences, freeway maps, architecture books, storybooks.

STORAGE

Items should be adjacent to area for block play or carrying carts should be available.

Shelves, baskets, boxes, cabinets, wood box on casters, labeled for organized storage.

Shelves should be open face for easy accessibility —division of shelves with boards helps keep like blocks together.

If material is stored outdoors, make sure it is protected from wet ground surfaces and damage from water play or rain.

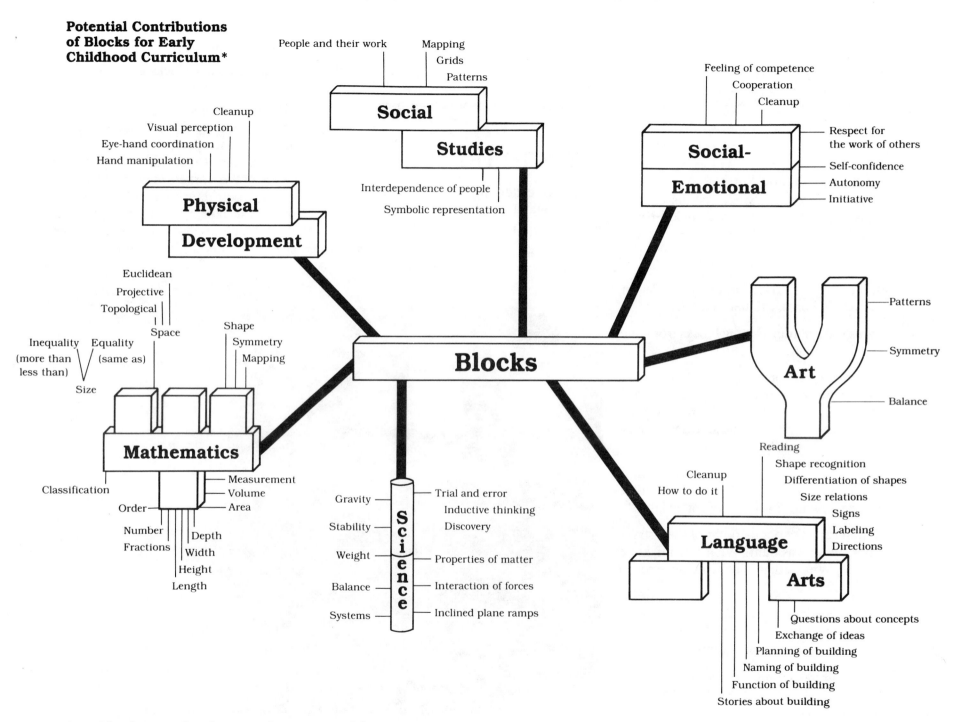

Potential Contributions of Blocks for Early Childhood Curriculum*

People and their work · Mapping · Grids · Patterns

Social Studies

Interdependence of people · Symbolic representation

Cleanup · Visual perception · Eye-hand coordination · Hand manipulation

Physical Development

Feeling of competence · Cooperation · Cleanup

Social-Emotional

Respect for the work of others · Self-confidence · Autonomy · Initiative

Euclidean · Projective · Topological · Space

Inequality (more than less than) · Equality (same as) · Size

Shape · Symmetry · Mapping

Blocks

Art

Patterns · Symmetry · Balance

Mathematics

Classification · Order · Number · Fractions · Width · Height · Length · Depth · Measurement · Volume · Area

Science

Gravity · Stability · Weight · Balance · Systems

Trial and error · Inductive thinking · Discovery · Properties of matter · Interaction of forces · Inclined plane ramps

Reading · Shape recognition · Differentiation of shapes · Size relations · Signs · Labeling · Directions

Cleanup · How to do it

Language Arts

Questions about concepts · Exchange of ideas · Planning of building · Naming of building · Function of building · Stories about building

***By Charlotte and Milton Brody. Reprinted from** The Block Book *(revised ed.) (1984) edited by Elisabeth S. Hirsch. National Association for the Education of Young Children, Washington, D.C.*

TOPICS TO TALK ABOUT WITH CHILDREN

Size, shape, and function—rectangular, triangular, cubical, spherical, cylindrical, circular, curve, elliptical curve, circular arch, small circle, ramps, buttress, floor board, pillar, Y switch, X switch, roofing boards, units, double units, quadruple units, Gothic arch, Gothic door.

Care and constructive use of blocks.

Determining best organization of blocks on shelves, in boxes, cabinets, baskets.

Various ways of transporting blocks from one area to another.

Children can plan for what is to be built: What blocks will be needed, what space is available, who will work with the blocks, how much time is there, what accessory materials are available?

Safety—can large blocks be perched on a small base? Is the available space adequate for the structure? Is it out of traffic lanes?

Children can take photographs of their structures. What was built? What else might be added? What other blocks or accessories might be used?

Children can develop new ideas on trips taken to see interesting buildings, freeways, lumberyards, construction equipment.

What are the economics and politics involved in construction? Discuss local problems and progress.

Explore the variety of occupations available in the construction industry. Talk with workers to learn more about how they fit into the total process.

IDEAS TO TRY

Encourage children to label buildings, numbers, street name, building name, etc.

Take trips to the lumberyard, brickyard, city hall, banks, markets, airport, department stores.

Children can sand blocks as needed to keep them free of splinters.

Initiate a discussion about new construction activity, and go for a walking trip. Take along a camera, steel tape measure, paper, pencils, and small rulers, tape recorder (some of the workers may agree to an interview). Upon returning, older children can make scale blueprints on graph paper, using their measurements of the construction site. Architects' blueprints, children's

There are times when everybody wants to help with the project; this creates opportunities for the children to share feelings of achievement, satisfaction, and cooperation.

sketches, and photographs can be displayed in the center. Encourage construction, story writing, and discussion about the project.

Revisit the site to observe progress. In this activity, children are:

- exploring concepts of size, shape, balance, length, width, volume, measurement, charting, and mapping.
- expanding language experience through story writing, problem solving, interviewing, and discussion.

- creating a personalized view of reality through construction and reproduction.
- mastering a task by undertaking a worthwhile project and seeing it through to completion.

Children may discover that the blocks on hand are not adequate for reproducing the desired construction. Extend the activity into the wood-working area, where the children can measure, saw, and sand their own blocks for completion of the project.

Resources

Berlfein, J. *A Classroom with Blocks* (Videotape). Washington, D.C.: National Association for the Education of Young Children, 1979.

Hirsch, E.S., ed. *The Block Book* (revised ed.). Washington, D.C.: National Association for the Education of Young Children, 1984.

Johnson, H.M. "The Art of Block Building." New York: Bank Street College of Education, 1933.

Rudolph, M., and Cohen, D.H. "The Many Purposes of Blockbuilding and Woodwork." *Young Children* 20, no. 1 (October 1964): 40–46.

Children enjoy improvising and may be motivated to do so through their own experiences, music, art, or a story which captures their attention.

Dramatic Play— Imagination—Drama

7

Dramatic play is a ticket to anywhere— the moon, a castle—it gives children a chance to step out of their own lives and become other people for a while. The shy, quite child can become a snarling lion in the wild animal show. The child who usually follows directions can become a construction supervisor, directing a large project. Dramatic play is fast-moving and original, managed by the children themselves. It stands magically apart from grownup's rules and schedules, yet gives children power to do all the things they see adults do: buying, selling, directing, traveling, rewarding, and punishing.

Dressing up in fancy clothes, such as ballet costumes, space helmets and goggles, floppy hats, and capes, is fun and lets children try things that might be scary in real life. Destroying snakes and monsters, whining and crying like a baby, or being mean mothers, fathers, or teachers, allows children to release strong feelings and express pressing needs to be powerful, aggressive, brave, strong, or helpless. Sometimes dramatic play is a good way to relive happy experiences, and sometimes it is a comforting way to make up for parts of a day that have not been so good.

Playing the youngest child in the family, the busy mother, or the tough police officer may help children see things from someone else's point of view and help them understand why people act the way they do. Playing newspaper reporters, gas station attendants, secretaries, or letter carriers helps children increase their understanding of what really happens in the grownup world. For example, they learn that reporters interview people and write stories. Coworkers take photographs, design layouts, print copy, and sell a finished product. Some kinds of dramatic play help children work through frightening, embarrassing, or unhappy experiences they have had and come to solutions that are helpful to them in facing similar situations.

Dramatic play sometimes requires groups of children to push heavy boxes or build up the fort or round up enough friends to make a patrol. This helps children learn that sometimes people need and depend on one another. It also helps children learn to work together: sharing, taking turns, dividing responsibilities, and accepting rules such as using words to express ideas, wants, plans, and feelings. It encourages children to learn more descriptive words and shows them that language is important if they want to be heard and understood.

Dramatic play not only provides opportunities for learning about unfamiliar situations, it also provides a unique opportunity for children to become more aware of themselves— their bodies, their thoughts, and their feelings. One way to open these avenues to children is through the use of creative dramatics.

Creative dramatics is a more mature form of the spontaneous dramatic play of young children. Group activities such as story improvisations, body movement, and pantomime give older children a chance to articulate their thoughts and feelings and to socialize and work together toward a common goal. These activities also stimulate ideas and creativity and give children experience in problem solving.

Children enjoy improvising and may be motivated to do so through their own experiences, music, art, or a story which captures their attention. The following suggestions may help you as you assist children in developing their improvisations.

You or one of the children may wish to select a story, to be either told or read by an adult or an older child. Care should be taken to select a clear and meaningful plot in which the characters are consistent and human. A limited number of incidents leading to a quick and satisfying ending would be best, especially for beginners. Older children can write their own stories.

Children can do much of the planning, character selection, and scene re-creation. Adults can be available to assist by asking questions to encourage children to expand their play. Individuals can be stimulated to think about their roles. For example, in a play about space travel, the adult can ask, "What happens to an astronaut when the spaceship blasts off? How would you hold your head? What would you do with your arms and legs? Have you seen videos of an astronaut walking on the moon? How does his body move? Are his steps short or long, fast or slow?"

Guidance may be necessary as each scene is developed. How does the scene start? What is the main conflict? What is each of the characters doing? What happened right before the scene began?

After the children have completed the improvisation, they may wish to discuss and evaluate it, possibly reading the story upon which it was based or writing to record dialogue and costumes used. Children can discuss their favorite parts, and may wish to relate the improvisation to situations they have encountered. Suggestions for improvements might be implemented.

EQUIPMENT AND MATERIALS

Children enjoy improvising and creativity can be stimulated by making a few materials available. You may wish to select a few items from these lists to encourage dramatic play.

General Learning Materials

Artificial flowers	Needles
Barrels	Oil cloth
Beads	Old lace curtains
Belts	Packing crates
Bits of bright fabrics	Pipe cleaners
Bits of leather	Planks (short and long)
Blocks	Plastic cloth
Boards	Props
Boxes	Purses
Buttons	Ribbons
Cargo nets	Sawhorses
Cheesecloth	Scarves
Cloth — assorted	Scissors
Coats	Sheets
Costumes	Shirts
Gloves	Shoes
Hats	Small mirrors
Horizontal ladders	Spools
Jewelry	Suspenders
Laces	Thread
Ladders	Tires
Long skirts	Tubes
Microphones	Wallets
Neckties	Yarn

Family

Brooms	Furniture
Cans of food	Lunch kits
Clock	Mixing spoons
Clothesline	Napkins
Clothespins	Plastic pans for washing
Dishes	babies or dishes
Dish towels	Pots and pans
Dolls	Suitcases
Dust pan	Tablecloths
Eating utensils	Telephones
Floor mops	Towels and washcloths

Medical

Adhesive tape	Lab coats
Admittance forms	Magazines
Aprons	Nurses' caps
Band-Aids™	Plastic hypos
Bottles	Stethoscopes
Doctor bag	Wagons
Flashlight	Watch
Gauze	

Office

Adding machine	Notepads
Briefcase	Order books
Calendars	Pencils
Cash register	Pens
Computer	Printing set
Drafting board	Stamps
Envelopes	Stapler
File	Telephone book
Hole puncher	Telephones
Manila folders	Typewriter
Material to file	Wastebasket

Camping

Back packs	
Barbecues	Hiking boots
Blankets	Lanterns
Canteens	Sleeping bags
Flash lights	Tents

Beautician

Bobby pins	Nail polish
Bottles	Oil for cuticles
Combs	Orange sticks
Cotton puffs	Plastic caps
Emery boards	Powder boxes
Hair clips	Rollers
Hand lotion	Soap
Hand mirror	Towels

Store

Baskets	Play money
Cash register	Scale
Items for sale	Shopping bags

Firefighter

Bell	Ladders
Hats	Wagons
Hose	Wheel

Gas Station

Cash register	Rags
Gas cans	Road maps
Gas pump	Steering wheel
Hose	Tire pump
Oil cans	Tool box
Play money	Tools

Bus or Train

Lunch box	Ticket punch
Money changer	Tickets
Newspaper	

Construction

Hose	Shovels
Pipes for water	Steamroller
Plastic buckets	Trucks
Rope and pulley	Wheelbarrow

STORAGE

Boxes, shelves, drawers, cabinets, baskets, hooks, all labeled to facilitate return and retrieval.

Items should be stored near the area in which they are most likely to be used; portable units may be necessary for some items.

Personal property in temporary use should be marked.

Portable Storage Unit

TOPICS TO TALK ABOUT WITH CHILDREN

Skills used in various dramatic play situations.

Originality, imagination, inventiveness— new ways of doing things, how people do things in different ways.

Props children can make themselves— puppet theater, puppets, dressup clothes, stage settings, costumes.

Items children can bring from home to supplement props for dramatic play and drama.

Stories, poems, books, pictures, films, filmstrips, television, and radio—what children watch and listen to at home and reenact at the center.

School trips to airports, railroad stations, firehouses, and theaters.

Freedoms and limitations—children's responsibilities to follow through on safety, care, and replacement of materials.

The children themselves—what they would enjoy doing, how they feel, places they have visited with their families, places they have lived, what they do on weekends.

People—where they work, what they do, how they dress, what they eat, how they play, where they live, how they are similar and different, how they are dependent on one another.

Current events—in the center, neighborhood, city, state, country, world—as they relate to children's play, interest, and understanding.

IDEAS TO TRY

Children can make hideouts, houses, tents, caves, forts, or stores from sheets, blankets, rugs, painter's drop clothes, tarpaulins.

Help children cut holes in cardboard boxes for crawl-through equipment. Cut top and bottom out of a large cardboard box and cut down on one side to make a four-panel screen; use as house, store, post office.

Old appliances and mechanical parts can be mounted on boards for use as control units, dashboards.

Spaceships can be made by children from tall fiberboard tubes with the nose cone from a sheet of lightweight cardboard. Cover windows with cellophane, transparent plastic wrap, tissue paper, or waxed paper. Five-gallon ice cream containers are perfect for space hats.

Stack tires for a hiding place or a house; make climbing equipment by tying three or four tires together side by side and then tying each end to a tree or post.

A trampoline can be constructed from a tire and canvas; stretch canvas taunt and carefully bolt to the tire.

Tree houses can be built by the children with different ways to get up and down: rope ladders, logs, boxes, planks, steps, rocks.

Wigs can be made from wool, raffia, and pulled crepe paper.

For original costumes, children can crayon designs on fabric and iron between sheets of absorbent paper.

Coins and money can be made from paper, cardboard, aluminum foil, papier-mâché, clay.

Paper flowers and papier-mâché jewelry can be made to sell in play stores; display in boxes, on shelves, on tables.

Have children plan a circus. Make pompoms, hats, costumes for a parade, masks, animal cages, banners. Sell popcorn, tickets.

Children can make musical instruments, march as a band, use a variety of instruments for an orchestra.

Make totem poles from cardboard boxes for a Native-American village; make clothing from unbleached muslin, headbands from leather, moccasins from leather, jewelry from clay. Join three poles together at top and cover with burlap bags to make a home.

Help children make street signs, signals, prices for merchandise, address signs.

Talk with parents about discarded items children can bring from home.

Visit gas stations for old tires and tubes; telephone company for telephones and large wire wheels from cables; television stores for large cardboard boxes and old television cabinets; aircraft salvage departments for a variety of mechanical devices, boxes, crates, cabinets, and parts; markets for crates, boxes, and posters.

Visit airline offices for maps, time schedules, hats, wings, and carry bags; furniture stores for rug samples, fabric samples, and packing crates; junkyards for gears, steering wheels, keys, and dashboards.

Children can construct a large animal from a sawhorse or by putting a log across two sawhorses. Add head, tail, and mane for a horse; carpet and upholstery samples to make a woolly sheep; horns or antlers to make a mythical beast.

Accompany a group of children to the library for selection of a play or a story they wish to enact.

Encourage older children to read to younger children and to help facilitate creative play.

Ask a local performer to demonstrate skills and assist children in their development.

Accompany a group of children to the theater.

Resources

Anderson, Y. *Make Your Own Animated Movies.* Boston: Little, Brown, 1970.

Chambers, D.W. *Storytelling and Creative Drama.* Dubuque, Iowa: William C. Brown, 1970.

Ehrlick, H., ed. *Creative Dramatics Handbook.* Urbana, Ill.: National Council of Teachers of English, 1974.

Gardner, R. *Costumes for All Ages, All Occasions.* New York: David McKay, 1970.

Gillies, E. *Creative Dramatics for Children.* Washington, D.C.: Association for Childhood Education International, 1973.

McCaslin, N. *Shows on a Shoestring.* New York: David McKay, 1979.

McVickar, P. *Imagination: Key to Human Potential.* Pasadena, Calif.: Pacific Oaks College Press, 1981.

Moncure, J.B. "Something Out of Nothing." *Young Children* 20, no. 1 (October 1964): 38–39.

Silks, G.B. *Drama with Children.* New York: Harper & Row, 1977.

Snook, B. *Costumes for Children.* Newton Centre, Mass.: Charles T. Branford, 1970.

Wels, B. *Magic.* New York: Putnam, 1967.

Williard, P. *Collecting Things.* New York: Doubleday, 1975.

Yerian, C., and Yerian, M., eds. *Fun Time Activities: Plays and Special Effects.* Chicago: Childrens Press, 1975.

Puppets, Marionettes, and Literature   8

Puppets are beautiful and fun to watch. Children putting on puppet shows hear their friends laughing and clapping, and they have a chance to feel successful, powerful, funny, and entertaining. Hidden by the curtain during a puppet show or just sitting on a rug playing with puppets, children create their own world of make-believe—"You be the frog and I'll be the princess." "I'm going to be silly." With puppets, children can do things that might be embarrassing or frightening in real life. For the children using the puppets as well as for the children watching, puppets are a ticket to a different world.

As they make puppets kick their legs, nod their heads, wave their arms, open their mouths, and whisk back and forth, children develop hand-eye coordination and learn to use their small muscles skillfully. Making puppets speak so the audience can hear and understand them helps children learn to speak clearly.

Carefully following the story and the action of the puppets requires children to learn to listen carefully. Acting the part of the shy, angry, silly, mean, kind, stuck-up, scared, or brave puppet gives children a chance to find out about their own and other people's feelings. It gives them a chance to test feelings and responses in different situations—"I'm scared so I'll hide." "I like you, so I'll hug you."

Playing with puppets and putting on shows gives children opportunities to work together and to solve problems—"You can come in after my puppet falls down." "How can we make a big enough stage for all of us to fit behind?" With puppets, children can make up stories from their own experiences. They also can be encouraged to read books, poems, and songs to get ideas to use with their puppets. Puppet shows to be presented before an audience give children the opportunity to learn how to plan for the time length of the show and for the beginning, the exciting part, and the end of the story. Children can write what everyone is going to say, and can make signs announcing the show. Some shows are made up as they go along instead of being carefully planned; in both kinds there are wonderful opportunities for children to imagine, to dream, to think about possibilities and realities, and then to put these ideas into words and actions that can be shared with others.

MATERIALS

Bags—all sizes
Balloons
Balls
Beads
Boxes—all shapes and sizes
Broom straws
Brushes—assorted sizes and shapes
Buttons, button molds
Cans—all sizes and shapes
Cardboard
Clay
Cloth—all colors, sizes, textures
Cork
Cotton batting
Crayons
Curtains and curtain rods
Doweling
Embroidery and sewing thread
Feathers

41

Felt
Felt pens
Foil
Gloves
Glue
Gourds
Hammer, nails, and screws
Handkerchiefs
Hooks and eyes, snaps
Jewelry
Kapok
Lace
Lace doilies
Leather
Magazines
Masonite™
Needles
Nylon hose
Paints—tempera and enamel
Paper—wrapping, cleansing tissue, construction, cardboard tubing and cones, contact, corrugated, gift wrap, graph, napkins, newspaper, telephone books, towel
Paper fasteners
Papier-mâché
Paste
Pencils
Pins
Pipe cleaners
Plastic wood
Plywood
Raffia
Ribbons
Rope
Rubber bands
Sawdust
Scissors
Screens
Shellac or lacquer
Shoelaces
Socks

Sponges
Spools
Stapler
Sticks
String—all colors and weights
Styrofoam
Tape
Tennis balls
Thumbtacks
Tongue depressors
Trimmings—all kinds
Tulle
Turpentine
Window shades
Wire—thin
Wire coathangers
Yardstick
Zippers

STORAGE

Boxes, shelves, baskets, cabinets, cupboards, drawers, labeled. Shelves of different heights and widths to accommodate puppets, marionettes, and accessory materials.

Acting the part of a puppet gives children a chance to find out about their own and other people's feelings.

Plastic bags, closed containers for puppets and marionettes, labeled.
Cardboard or cloth hanging shoe organizers.
Cardboard or plastic shoe boxes.

TOPICS TO TALK ABOUT WITH CHILDREN

Which kind of puppet or marionette would best fit the character?

How to care for puppets and marionettes.

Color, size, shape, texture, and other variations of materials which can be used for making puppets, marionettes, and stages.

Books, stories, poetry, and songs that can be reenacted with puppets and marionettes.

How to manipulate puppets and marionettes to create the story and express feeling.

Integration of the many media needed for puppetry.

Children can develop plans for coordination of characters, language, setting, scenery.

Trips to puppet shows at public libraries or amusement parks.

IDEAS TO TRY

Design and make many different kinds of puppets—paper bag, stick, rod, shadow, cardboard, sock, glove, finger, folded paper, handkerchief or other cloth over fist, twig, box, felt.

Design and make marionettes using a variety of materials for head and bodies—papiermâché, crushed paper, styrofoam, wood, boxes of all sizes and shapes, clay, stocking over kapok, hinged or strung.

Design and make costumes utilizing art and sewing skills.

Observe and design puppets and costumes that represent community workers, fantasy people and animals, storybook figures, circus clowns and animals, ethnic groups.

Develop original dialogue or use a favorite story or poem as a base.

Plan and make props, stage scenery for puppet theater.

Design and make a puppet theatre. It can be impromptu or more permanent, simple or complex. Use carpentry tools.

Sew curtains and develop ways to open and close curtains.

Make storage boxes for puppets, marionettes, costumes, props, etc.

Plan and make posters for publicity for puppet presentation, using creative art experiences.

Take trips to commercial puppet theaters; see amateur performances at schools, community playgrounds, and libraries.

Resources

Batchelder, M.H. *The Puppet Theatre Handbook*. New York: Harper & Row, 1974.

Batchelder, M.H., and Comer, V.L. *Puppets and Plays: A Creative Approach*. New York: Harper & Row, 1956.

Bates, E. *Potpourri of Puppetry*. Canyon, Texas: West Texas State University, 1974.

Howard, V. *Puppet and Pantomime Plays*. New York: Sterling, 1971.

Mahlmann, L., and Jones, D.C. *Puppet Plays for Young Players*. Boston: Plays, 1974.

The center day can begin and end with music. Small groups of children and staff may gather informally for a round of favorite songs.

Music, Movement, and Dance

The special joys of music and dance should be a part of each day for children. Music offers so many things—the pleasure of singing favorite songs with friends or of musing and dreaming while listening to a record, the exhilaration of folk dances, the excitement of creating one's own dance. Music is a wonderful outlet for feelings of joy, sorrow, or anger. It encourages children to express their feelings creatively and gives them a sense of belonging.

The center day can begin and end with music. Small groups of children and staff may gather informally for a round of favorite songs. Accompaniment is not essential; if a staff member or older child can play the piano, guitar, or other instrument, this adds to the enjoyment. Children and adults can quickly learn to accompany themselves on an autoharp.

Every child has favorite songs and keeps adding to the collection: songs that tickle the funny bone—"I Know an Old Lady Who Swallowed a Fly"; songs that quicken a sense of beauty—"Oh, How Lovely Is the Evening"; or songs that start the child off on a lively march—"Stars and Stripes Forever."

Music of different cultures and countries should be part of each child's experience. Folk songs and dances from around the world provide a natural outlet for children's expanding interest in other people and countries; melodies and rhythms have universal appeal.

Children's ears are tuned to the beat of rock and soul music, and to exclude this form of contemporary musical expression from the center would be a denial of an important part of their environment. It is good for children to have a chance to compare many kinds of musical expression. Ask children to share their favorite rock songs with you; meanwhile, listen to the radio yourself. Capitalize on children's fervent interest in contemporary rock music and use it in many ways.

Language learnings in music are evident in expanded vocabularies. The more children sing, the better they may read, speak, and listen. Older children can read directions for making instruments and can be helpful to younger children.

Hand in hand with singing goes dance. There should be opportunities for many kinds of body movement experiences in the all-day program. The familiar pleasures of folk dancing should be balanced with chances to explore other ways of moving arms and legs and bodies. Encourage children to use the tom-tom to create rhythmic patterns which will lead them to create their own dances. Dance with them and encourage them to respond to rhythm and music in their own unique manner. You will not need many props—plenty of space, indoors and out, and a tom-tom will suffice to begin with. Later on, you can add some of the accessories suggested; hoops to roll and scarves or crepe paper streamers to twirl are especially versatile for children.

The more children move, the better they move; the better they know what they can do with their bodies, the better they use their bodies to communicate feelings and ideas. And they love doing it.

When children get excited about music, it spills over into the whole program. Soon they will be creating their own rhythm instruments and their own songs. Parents will catch this excitement, too. Late afternoon sings can be family affairs, with parents joining in as they arrive to pick up their children. Many parents have musical talents; a visit from a parent to share and play an instrument or to sing is a never-to-be-forgotten treat and a wonderful way of learning about music.

It is important to have good commercial musical instruments and equipment so that children can learn to recognize fine tone quality. Whether children use commercial instruments or create their own, the following criteria apply:

- Instruments should have good tone quality so that they make a real musical contribution, not just noise.
- Instruments should be attractive and durable.
- Instruments from various cultural groups should be as authentic as possible.

The familiar pleasures of folk dancing should be balanced with chances to explore other ways of moving arms and legs and bodies.

46

EQUIPMENT

Autoharp
Bells—sleigh bells, temple bells, jingle bells, wrist bells, resonator bells
Books—poetry, song, and story
Cassettes
Castanets
Chinese temple blocks
Clogs
Cymbals—hand and finger
Drums—Native American, bongo, floor, hand rhythm, tom-tom
Films and filmstrips
Guitar
Maracas and maraca sticks
Piano
Pictures
Record player
Records—classical, ethnic, holiday, marches, movement, singing, rhythm instruments, rock, contemporary, soul
Recorders
Rhythm sticks—wooden, bamboo, some fringed at ends
Tambourines
Tape recorder and tapes
Triangle and striker

MATERIALS

Balloons
Balls—light and heavy
Cloth—various sizes, shapes, and textures
Dressup clothes
Hoops
Pompoms
Ribbons
Ropes—clothesline, jump rope
Scarves
Streamers

STORAGE

Labeled boxes, bags, and baskets which can be used indoors or outdoors.

Pegboard and hooks for rhythm instruments, dressup clothing, hoops.

Portable labeled shelving units that can be moved about the room or pushed out of the way.

Clothesline and clothespins for hanging up costumes.

Record cabinet in which records are organized for quick selection.

Music books on specially marked bookshelves.

Picture file organized for easy access.

TOPICS TO TALK ABOUT WITH CHILDREN

Body balance—what happens when the child stands or hops on one foot or leans forward or backward or far to the side.

Differentiating sounds—the sound of a slight pounding of a drum and a large bang.

Feelings children experience when they hear soft, loud, fast, or slow music; lullabies; marches. How people feel and express their feelings through different media and in different ways.

Listening—following directions in making instruments, identifying types of sounds or instruments, learning words and melodies of new songs.

Choosing which songs to sing, records to play, materials to use.

Names, uses, categories, sounds, and parts of instruments; functions of parts of a record player; looking at the vibrating strings of a piano.

Care of instruments. Which ones require special efforts?

New sounds heard on the way to school or on the way home or on a visit. What do these sounds tell you?

Folk dances children enjoy doing. What do they mean to the cultures from which they come?

IDEAS TO TRY

Draw to different kinds of music.

Listen to lullabies and marches, ethnic folk music, restful music, music for movement and rhythm instruments.

Move to sounds of drums and rattles, combining movement with playing instruments and singing.

Use good rhythm instruments to develop musical appreciation. Have fun making music and doing body movements with child-made instruments—shakers, drums, tambourines, rhythm sticks, fringed bamboo sticks—and with simple instruments like castanets.

Use props for enhancing movement. Find different ways to use materials and equipment such as balls, balloons, streamers, and scarves.

Tap drum to sound like thunder and then tap to sound like falling rain.

Tape rhythm sticks together, tap sticks on floor, rug, wood, metal, cloth, tambourine.

When children get excited about music, it spills over into the whole program. Soon they will be creating their own rhythm instruments and their own songs.

Try moving body to poetry—running, leaping, skipping, walking slowly or rapidly, sliding, twisting, twirling.

Create tunes, songs, movement actions in many different ways.

Try sounds out on the piano; watch the hammers move as keys are struck.

Make up new sounds, new ways to move. Combine sounds and movement in ways you think will be fun.

47

Try to recognize instruments being used in records you are playing.

Take turns playing instruments, clapping while others play or dance.

Make a scrapbook of pictures—instruments, dancing, musical centers visited, concert halls, open air dances.

Accompany children to various performances—concerts, recitals, musicals. Discuss different types of music and dance and what moods are created by them.

Support children in their planning and implementing a talent show.

Encourage children to take dancing or instrumental lessons at their schools and to share their talents with the other children.

Assist children if necessary in writing their own music or creating their own interpretive dance.

Have children perform original compositions and choreograph dances.

Explore communication through pantomime.

Ask people in various music careers to visit the center, or visit them while they are at work—concert musicians, record store clerks, dancers at rehearsals, disc jockeys, composers.

Create a special, quiet place for listening.

Use such works as "Carnival of the Animals" and "Peter and the Wolf," expanding the children's musical interests and allowing for creative interpretation of the stories told by music.

Encourage children to really listen to music, rather than playing it as "background noise" which is soon ignored.

Play games with the instruments. For example, children can close their eyes or turn their backs while another child plays various instruments. The children identify which instrument is making the sound.

Rhythm Sticks

Sand two pieces of doweling, ¾″ × 7″ long. Paint, add an eye screw on one end of each piece and join with ribbon or braided yarn. Or cut two pieces of ½″ × 12″ doweling. A few notches cut into the doweling add to the interesting rhythm sounds. Sticks may be painted.

Sound Shakers

Sound shakers may be made from baby food cans or tomato sauce cans. Remove top and bottom portions of can; a stone may be used to smooth any rough edges. The can may be painted or covered for decoration. Cut dowel ¾″ × 4″ and sand one end. Punch a hole in the side of the can and attach the dowel with a wood screw; a small hole in the center of the dowel end will be helpful. Cut two pieces of used drumheads (contact school music departments) or inner tubes in 4″ circles. Punch holes in tube or drumhead 1″ apart and ¼″ from edge. Place on either end of the can and lace with yarn or string or ribbon. Before closing, insert various objects for different kinds of sounds.

Drums

Drums can be made by taping together three cans or boxes of the same or different sizes. Raffia, yarn, tape, ribbon, string, or plastic lacing; paint; crayons; finger paints; collage; contact paper; and wrapping paper may be used to add to the attractiveness of the drums.

Drum Beaters

Doweling and old tennis balls make good drum beaters. Punch a hole in the ball and push a piece of doweling into the center. Glue the end of doweling that goes into the ball.

Tapping Rhythm Instruments

Two stones, palm size, are useful as tapping rhythm instruments. Stones may be painted and shellacked.

Tambourines

Paste three paper plates together for firmness. Paint or collage with pieces of tissue paper, then shellac. Punch holes about 1″ apart and ½″ from the rim. Pound bottle tops flat and punch hole near the top of the caps. Tie bottle caps (two together) to the plates with string, yarn, or ribbon and shake—tambourines for dancing.

Jingle Sticks

With old-fashioned clothespins (found in hobby shops), you can make jingle sticks. It is also possible to use doweling or cut pieces of old broom handles. Pound a flat-headed nail through several buttons with large holes into the clothespin, leaving some space so that the buttons can jingle. Bottle tops can also be used—pound them flat, punch holes into the centers, and attach them to the clothespin like the buttons.

Shaker Bells

Shaker bells are made with 7″ long doweling or broomstick pieces. Cut a coathanger 15″ and make a slight arch. String bells on yarn or plastic lacing and wind around the hanger wire. Put an eye screw on each end of the wood; poke each end of the wire through the eye hook and bend back, clamping tight with a pincher. Colorful yarn or ribbons may be added to each end. Hands hold the wooden part for shaking.

Resources

Arnold, A. *The World Book of Children's Games.* New York: Fawcett World Publishing, 1975.

Barlin, A., and Barlin, P. *The Art of Learning Through Movement.* Los Angeles: Ward Ritchie Press, 1971.

Bartal, L., and Ne'eman, V. *Movement Awareness and Creativity.* New York: Harper & Row, 1975.

Blitner, J. *Hop, Skip, Jump, Read.* Long Beach, Calif.: Christian Press, 1972.

Burnett, M. *Dance Down the Rain, Sing up the Corn: American Indian Chants and Games.* Music Innovations, Box One, Allison Park, Pa. 15101, 1975.

Corbin, C.B. *Inexpensive Equipment for Games, Play, and Physical Activities.* Dubuque, Iowa: William C. Brown, 1972.

Ferretti, F. *The Great American Book of Sidewalk, Stoop, Dirt, Curb and Alley Games.* New York: Workman Publishing Co., 1975.

Forte, I., and Frank, M. *Puddles and Wings and Grapevine Swings.* Nashville, Tenn.: Incentive Publications, 1982.

Hawkinson, J., and Faulhaber, M.F. *Music and Instruments for Children To Make.* Chicago: Albert Whitman, 1969.

International Council on Health, Physical Education, and Recreation. *ICHPER Book of Worldwide Games and Dances.* Washington, D.C.: American Association for Health, Physical Education, and Recreation, 1967.

Joyce, M. *First Steps in Teaching Creative Dance to Children* (second ed.). Mountain View, Calif.: Mayfield Publications, 1980.

Langstaff, N., and Langstaff, J. *Jim Along Josie: A Collection of Folk Songs and Singing Games.* New York: Harcourt Brace Jovanovich, 1970.

Langstaff, J., and Langstaff, C. *Shimmy Shimmy Coke-Ca-Pop: City Children's Street Games and Rhymes.* New York: Doubleday, 1973

Millen, N. *Children's Games From Many Lands.* New York: Friendship Press, 1965.

Nelson, E. *Dancing Games for Children of All Ages.* New York: Sterling, 1978.

Nelson, E. *Movement Games for Children of All Ages.* New York: Sterling, 1975.

Prieto, M. *Play It in Spanish: Spanish Games and Folk Songs for Children.* New York: John Day Company, 1973.

Saffran, R.B. *First Books of Creative Rhythms.* New York: Holt, Rinehart and Winston, 1963.

Stinson, S.W. "Movement as Creative Interaction With the Child." *Young Children* 32, no. 6 (September 1977): 49–53.

Sullivan, M. *Feeling Strong, Feeling Free: Movement Exploration for Young Children.* Washington, D.C.: National Association for the Education of Young Children, 1982.

Werner, P.H., and Simmons, R.A. *Inexpensive Physical Equipment for Children.* Minneapolis, Minn.: Burgess, 1976.

Wolff, M. *The Kids' After School Activity Book.* Belmont, Calif.: David S. Lake, 1985.

Worstell, E.V. *Jump the Rope Jingles.* New York: Macmillan, 1961.

Sewing, knitting, and weaving are challenging for children, offering them pleasure, a sense of accomplishment, and a good bit of pride.

50

Stitchery, Weaving, Quilting, and Knitting 10

Sewing, knitting, quilting, and weaving are challenging and worthwhile for children—whether it is using basic stitches to make costumes or butterfly nets, or knitting a whole row without dropping any stitches. Children can create neckties, wall hangings, place mats, puppets, rugs, and scarves with their personal choice of color, shape, texture, and design. They can use these things themselves or proudly give them away as gifts. Children can rub cool smooth satin scraps or velveteen across their cheeks and imagine grandly with scraps of gold or silver braid. Sewing, weaving, and knitting create opportunities for children to be in the warm leisurely company of others of all ages, equally busy with similar projects.

Sewing, knitting, quilting, and weaving are excellent activities to develop hand-eye coordination and the precise, accurate use of small muscles as children work to thread the tiny eye of a needle or try to stitch a straight line or thread a leather thong through a pouch. These crafts encourage children to decide on a goal, then figure out what has to be done each step of the way (for example, measuring to see how long a shirt should be, then cutting the material, sewing it together, and hemming it). This is one way children can learn how to plan, solve problems, and figure out how the parts of something go together to make the whole. By measuring an inch of weaving or a yard of material, by using fat and skinny knitting needles or large darning needles and small sewing needles, by saying to themselves, "*Now* I'll cut it out," "*Later* I can put buttons on it," "*After the weekend* I can work on it again," "*One month from now* I can give it to my mother," children can connect real situations and real objects with abstract ideas such as time, length, and size.

As they knit, weave, and sew, children can practice arithmetic operations (for example, subtracting how much of the doll sweater is already knitted from the total length to figure out how many more rows there are to do). Wrestling with pattern and knitting directions gives children excellent practice in reading. They also learn new words by handling and naming materials and equipment: cotton, velvet, oilcloth, cheesecloth, looms, shuttles. Children learn to use language to share ideas, feelings, and information as they work.

Design and beauty are apparent as children decide for themselves why some combinations of color, shape, and texture seem beautiful while others do not, and see that not all people like the same combinations. Children can discover things about the creative arts (for example, the importance of costuming for mood and effect in creative dramatics, puppet shows, and dance). Children can also begin to see the relationships between size, weight, and function (for example, heavy materials make costumes that are hot to wear, darning needles make holes too big for ordinary sewing).

Knitting, sewing, quilting, and weaving are useful crafts—the pot holder can be used to pick up the hot pan or take the cookie sheet from the oven. There are opportunities for children to learn craft techniques used by our ancestors and still used by some people today. Elderly people in the community may especially find it meaningful to share their skills with children eager to learn new techniques.

can highlight personal tastes and interests, and signature squares give each contributor recognition. Quilting can produce impressive objects for gifts such as a pillow or tote bag. More ambitious, long-range projects can produce a jacket or a bolero. An old-fashioned quilting bee could involve mothers and older siblings and would be a good setting for conversation and discussion.

Sewing, weaving, and knitting create opportunities for children to be in the warm leisurely company of others of all ages, equally busy with similar projects.

In addition, these crafts encourage children to be responsible for their own products and for the care of equipment, tools, and supplies; to see the relationship between safety and responsibility—pins and needles need to be returned to pincushions or proper boxes, scissors should be carried with the points down.

Quilting has returned as a popular craft. For many reasons, it is an ideal activity for the later school-age years, both for individual children and as a group activity. As quilts have emerged on the national scene as symbols—for peace, for example—techniques of quilting have been made clearer and simpler. Using a sewing machine will complete a quilting project faster than sewing everything by hand. A group could piece a quilt, with each child contributing a square about an interest (sports, music, pets) or a local interest or fad. Piecing and embroidering

EQUIPMENT

Embroidery hoops
Hammer and nails
Knitting needles
Looms—various sizes and shapes
Needles—needles with large holes, large needles for thicker cotton thread and yarn, blunt needles for stitchery
Sewing machine

MATERIALS

Cloth—variety of sizes, shapes, colors, textures, i.e., cotton, flannel, burlap, felt, silk, satin, brocade
Clotheshangers or dowelings for hangings
Dye—various colors
Kapok
Patterns
Pins and pincushions
Picture frames—to use as looms or for framing pictures stitched on cloth
Scissors and pinking shears
Shuttles—can be made from cardboard
Snaps, hooks and eyes
Spool with tacks for knitting chains of yarn

52

String, cord, and fine wire
Tape measure
Thimbles
Thread—various colors, #50 and for embroidery
Tracing wheel and paper
Trimmings, bias tape, ribbons, buttons, braid, rickrack
Yarn

STORAGE

Boxes or drawers for different size materials and supplies, labeled.

Shopping bags, baskets, sewing boxes.

Shoe boxes—cardboard or clear plastic.

Egg cartons or muffin tins for small items, such as hooks and eyes, snaps.

Empty cardboard tubes or spools for winding on ribbons, braid, etc., when not in use.

Patterns and directions for each activity stored with the materials and equipment needed—knitting needles, yarn, and directions together; embroidery hoops, silk, thread, cloth, and stitch patterns together.

Safe place where a child can store a project while still working on it.

TOPICS TO TALK ABOUT WITH CHILDREN

Materials needed—cloth, yarn, scissors, needles (sewing, knitting), hoops—to complete a project.

Sizes, shapes, textures, colors, weights, and various materials.

Sequence in the development of sewing, quilting, or weaving an item.

Size of needles and thread needed for various activities.

Safety rules about putting needles in pincushions, carrying scissors.

How materials and supplies will be organized and stored when not in use.

Kinds of costumes needed for dramatic play.

How looms are designed and built, new vocabulary of warp and woof.

How stores select clothing for sale.

How dye is made and used.

Handicrafts of ethnic groups.

Proper use of sewing machine.

IDEAS TO TRY

Dye cloth or yarn, make dye colors from vegetables, crepe paper, inks.

Knit a variety of items—scarves, doll sweaters, booties, hats, rugs, ties, belts.

Learn a variety of stitches for hand sewing.

Make original designs and sew costumes.

Make hanks of yarn into balls for looms, yarn dolls and animals, etc.

Make looms of various sizes and shapes; compare resulting products.

Make shuttles for weaving from tongue depressors, cardboard, balsa wood.

Younger children can experience success in making simple items such as pot holders and hand puppets.

Take trips to stores—clothing stores, gift shops, stitchery and yard good shops, sew-

Sewing, knitting, quilting, and weaving are excellent activities to develop hand-eye coordination and the precise, accurate use of small muscles.

ing factories, 5 and 10 cent stores. Write about and illustrate the experiences.

Make wall hangings using coathangers, cloth, doweling, string. (See Chapter 5.)

Experiment with various cords and yarn for macrame.

Sew curtains, hats, purses, clothing, handkerchiefs, laundry bags, slippers, doll clothing, stuffed animals, pillows.

53

Sew samplers, Christmas stockings, other holiday gifts.

Sew sit-upons, i.e., oilcloth cover over newspapers, punch holes along outside, and sew together with blunt needles and yarn.

Younger children enjoy burlap and yarn stitchery with large needles.

Sewing hints — Help children learn to use a thimble on the middle finger. Start with simple stitches and add stitches as need and interest are indicated:

1. *Running stitch:* Run the threaded needle in and out of the cloth in a straight or curved line. Take only two or three stitches before pulling the needle through. Stitches and spaces should be even.

2. *Basting stitch:* Same as running stitch except the stitches are larger.

3. *Overcast stitch or whipstitch:* Work from front to back over edge of fabric. This stitch is used to keep edges of seams together and to keep material from raveling.

4. *Backstitch:* Gives the effect of machine stitching but is done by hand. Take one stitch backward. Bring the needle up through the material a stitch ahead of where you started. Take another backstitch meeting the last stitch and once more bring the needle up through the material a stitch ahead of where you started. A combination of backstitch and running stitch can be used when there is a large area to cover. Take two or three backstitches and then two or more running stitches.

54

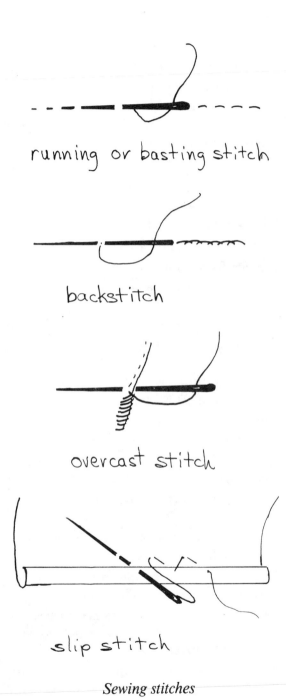

running or basting stitch

backstitch

overcast stitch

slip stitch

Sewing stitches

5. *Slip stitch:* Usually used for hemming. Stitches are fine and should not show through on the right side. From the other side, pick up two or three threads of material with the threaded needle, then insert needle into the edge of the folded hem and pull the needle through. Continue alternating in this manner, being sure that all the stitches are the same size and the same width apart.

Beanbags — Cut two pieces of felt, heavy ticking, or other tightly woven material. Shapes may be round, square, oblong, shaped like turtles, owls, penguins, etc. Sew together, leaving opening at one end. Turn inside out; pour beans or rice through a funnel into the opening; sew; decorate.

Other projects — Try weaving — cloth, basket, or paper; patchwork quilting; appliqué; stuffed dolls, pillows, or animals; needlepoint; rug hooking; crochet; macrame.

Resources

Green, S. *Patchwork for Beginners.* New York: Watson-Guptill, 1973.

Ickis, M., ed. *Handicrafts and Hobbies.* New York: Greystone, 1948.

Kroncke, G. *Simple Weaving: Designs, Material, Technique.* Cincinnati, Ohio: Van Nostrand Reinhold, 1973.

Lightbody, D. *Easy Weaving.* New York: Lothrop, Lee & Shepard, 1974.

Rush, B. *The Stitchery Idea Book.* Cincinnati, Ohio: Van Nostrand Reinhold, 1974.

Seward, L. *The Complete Book of Patchwork, Quilting and Appliqué.* Englewood Cliffs, New Jersey: Prentice-Hall, 1987.

Construction/ Carpentry

11

By learning to use real tools and methods, school-age children can build things that are impressive and useful—everything from airplanes, wagons, and puppet theaters to elaborate wood sculptures.

They can create, imagine, invent, and decorate. As they cut with saws, pry out nails with a hammer, open the jaws of a wrench, or adjust a vise, children can discover many things. They can find out that lumber is cut from trees, that houses and furniture and stairs and boxes are made by real people, that objects do not ordinarily stand up or stick together but must be arranged to balance and be joined by nails or glue. Working with wood helps children feel a kinship with carpenters and other adult builders who work with wood.

By lugging heavy boards, shaping balsa wood into airplanes and tossing them lightly to the wind, tracing the grain of a plank, and smoothing away splinters and rough edges, children can apply such abstract concepts as weight, size, length, texture, color, and variety to objects from their own world. Children can see the results and importance of mathematical operations such as addition, subtraction,

By learning to use real tools and methods, children can build things that are impressive and useful.

55

and reversibility—a carefully measured and cut lid really fits its box.

Woodworking develops hand-eye coordination and large and small muscles. As they work, children find it easy to talk with other children about tools, to share ideas, projects, and materials, and to discuss what they are learning to do. Older children may find that younger children appreciate their assistance as they learn new skills. This kind of conversation and cooperation generates good feelings. Woodworking presents problems to be solved, it demands stick-to-it-iveness, and it requires that safety precautions and responsibility for tools be recognized. Working with wood also encourages children to develop good work habits as they plan how to carry out projects and cooperate with other children. What marvelous opportunities for growth woodworking offers to children!

EQUIPMENT

All tools should be real, adult, good quality tools, not toys.

Awl
Brace (drill) and wood bits—6-8″ sweep
C-clamps
File
Hammers—11 to 13 oz., bent claw with drop-forged heads
Knife—utility
Plane
Pliers
Rasp—medium bite, 10″ long
Safety blocks
Sawhorses

Saws—coping (6″ blades), cross-cut (16-20″, good steel), keyhole, rip
Scissors
Screwdrivers—regular and Phillips, short, heavy handled
T-square
Tape measure
Tin snips
Vise
Workbench or table
Wrench—adjustable

MATERIALS

Aprons with pockets
Glue
Graph paper
Hole punch
Leather pieces
Marking pens
Magnets
Nails—assorted sizes
Paint—water based and enamel
Paint brushes
Pencils
Rags
Rulers
Sandpaper—#1 to #00, wrap around a small block
Screws—wood, flat and round heads
Screw eyes and hooks
Shellac
String
Tacks
Turpentine
Varnish
Washers
Wire
Wood—soft pine, poplar, plywood, balsa, doweling—various sizes
Yardsticks

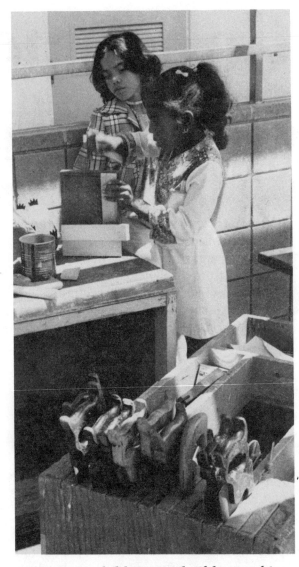

School-age children can build everything from airplanes, wagons, and puppet theaters to elaborate wood sculptures.

STORAGE

Barrels, boxes, garbage cans, or wastepaper baskets for wood and other materials.

Muffin tins, small plastic containers, or shoe boxes for nails, screws, tacks, etc.

Shelving for projects in process.

Tools should be hung whenever possible to avoid damage. Pegboards marked with the location of each tool are best. Small items such as clamps can be stored in boxes or drawers. All storage should be labeled and located in the woodworking area.

TOPICS TO TALK ABOUT WITH CHILDREN

How to use each tool, including safety precautions. Have a first aid kit readily available.

How to care for tools—tools should be hung in a dry place, saws sharpened regularly, hammer handles checked for cracks.

How to combine materials such as wood and nails or wood and glue.

Why sandpapering items is sometimes necessary for painting readiness or for safety.

Ideas to enable easier movement—add wheels to a box.

The process of making lumber from trees.

Pulling out nails so they won't bend; use a small wood block under hammerhead.

Hammer holding—grasp hammer near the end of the handle, not close to the head. Hit nail sharply.

Planes are used for smoothing and scraping wood. Hold plane with knob forward, push forward with the grain of the wood, holding one hand on knob, the other on the handle. Wood should be firmly clamped to table or workbench.

Children should use a coping saw with even, vertical strokes and without too much pressure. To cut a circle, drill a hole at some point on the circle, remove one end of blade from the saw, pass the blade through the drilled hole. Reclamp blade in the frame and saw.

IDEAS TO TRY

Children can design and build games— beanbag stand, ring toss stand, floor checkerboard.

Older children may wish to design and build equipment for dramatic play—stove, refrigerator, sink, shelves.

Wood marionettes are a special challenge.

Design and build a puppet theater; coordinate project with puppet makers, playwrights, and set designers.

Older children may find that younger children appreciate their assistance as they learn new skills. This kind of conversation and cooperation generates good feelings.

Accessory materials can be constructed for block play.

Wood boxes could be made for special uses— toys, blocks, cubbies.

A box with wheels can be hooked to a wagon, trike, or bike.

Build simple bookcases for storage.

Table dollhouses can be made from boxes; simple dollhouse furniture can also be constructed.

Use children's skills to repair equipment— sandpaper rough blocks, pound in nails, glue and clamp a broken drawer.

Sandpaper, paint, and decorate completed items such as boats and planes.

Discuss trips taken and career possibilities. Take trips to cabinet shops, lumber mills, furniture factories and stores, paint shops, hardware stores, buildings being constructed. Invite others in the community to assist children as they work.

Racing Boats

Wood scraps	Paint and/or varnish
Popsicle sticks	Sandpaper
Rubber bands	Graph paper, rulers, compasses, etc.

Adults or older children can explain the basic design and discuss the way in which the boat works. The children can then create a pattern for their boat on graph paper and decide which wood pieces and tools they will need. Individually labeled boxes for storing unfinished projects will be necessary as construction may take several days.

Resources

Alton, W.G. *Wooden Toys That You Can Make.* New York: Taplinger, 1972.

Brandhofer, M. "Carpentry for Young Children." *Young Children 27,* no. 1 (October 1971): 17–23.

Cleaver, D. *The Box Book.* New York: David McKay, 1974.

Skeen, P.; Garner, A.P.; and Cartwright, S. *Woodworking for Young Children.* Washington, D.C.: National Association for the Education of Young Children, 1983.

Thompson, D. *Woodstuff for Kids.* Mt. Rainier, Maryland: Gryphon House, 1981.

Activities With Water

12

Water is a source of pleasure to children of all ages. It feels and usually looks and sounds good—cool and refreshing, smooth and soapy, warm and relaxing. It is a natural material without uses that have been predetermined by a manufacturer. A child's imagination can change water into almost anything—paint, coffee, fire-extinguishing fluid, cakes, chocolate, the ocean. This opens wide the door to the joy of discovery. It creates opportunities for many kinds of play, including messy play with sand and mud which are such fun and so important for children. Water alone and water combined with sand and mud are materials children of all ages can use. They are not products which must fit someone else's standards.

Children can learn a great deal from working and playing with water and observing how it looks and what it can do. Using water, children can do the things adults do—such as cooking, washing, mixing paints. They can be firefighters, plumbers, or painters for the moment and develop kinship with the adults in the community who actually do these jobs.

As children play with water, sand, and mud, they can find out about absorption, evaporation, floating, freezing, melting, dissolving. They build language skills by adding these and other relevant words (such as *wading, sprinkling, stirring, faucet, spigot, siphon*) to their vocabularies. Through measuring, pouring, hauling, running through, building dams for, and swimming in water, children can sharpen hand-eye coordination and develop both large and small muscles. Cleanup and toileting routines, fish-tank cleaning, animal feeding, and plant-growing projects can teach children about personal hygiene, their own physical needs, and the physical needs of other living things. Children can also learn about safety firsthand—staying out of deep water when swimming, taking turns in the sprinkler. In each of these water activities, observation, organization, problem solving, mastery of skills, and responsibility for protecting, caring for, and preserving materials are important. In all of these ways children learn to better understand themselves and the world around them.

Careful conservation of water is now a necessity, and in some areas water play activities may have to be curtailed if community supplies are low. To eliminate wasteful uses of water, provide basins or tubs for water play—eliminate the use of running water. Unless water is soapy, it can be used to water plants either indoors or out once it is no longer suitable for play. Soapy water might by used to wash riding toys, to clean doll clothes, or to scrub the sidewalk. Just as children can be creative in using water they can be creative in conserving this precious natural resource.

EQUIPMENT

Aprons (waterproof)
Aquarium
Basins, tubs, pails
Bubble pipes
Cylinders — graduated sizes, metric markings
Garden hoses
Kitchen utensils — eggbeaters, sieves, measuring cups, pitchers, baster, muffin tins, funnels, spray bottles
Plastic bottles — various sizes and shapes
Plastic runners
Sandbox

MATERIALS

Boats
Brushes
Food coloring
Liquid soap
Rags
Sponges
Straws

STORAGE

Barrels, boxes, or baskets for small items, near place where they will be used with water.
Sheds for outdoor equipment.
Plastic bags for small water toys.
Chicken wire over the sandbox to discourage cats.

Water, sand, and mud are materials children of all ages can use. They are not products which must fit someone else's standards.

TOPICS TO TALK ABOUT WITH CHILDREN

Discuss how water sustains life — of people, pets, wild animals, birds, plants, trees.

Occupations related to water — firefighting, farming, plumbing, fishing, carwashing, street cleaning, lifeguarding, window washing, engineering, resource management, utilities.

Visit the beach, lakes, rivers; a fish hatchery, dam, marina; fire station; car wash. Discuss how water affects our lives. Children may wish to write stories.

Children can experiment with many forms of water — icicles, ice cubes, Popsicles, snow, steam, dew, hail, rain, frost; how water expands when it freezes, mixes with some things but not with others, has air in it, can be absorbed, can change in form.

Discuss why some things sink in water and others float. Why does a nail sink but an oceanliner float?

Explore dams and their functions.

Exercise water safety. All swimming activities should be carefully supervised. What should children know if they are on a boat?

Try new words — *erosion, displacement, absorption, porosity, saturation.*

Older children may wish to pursue water management in their area. Who is responsible? Where are reserves stored?

As children become aware of the relationship between rain, water storage, commercial and personal use, they can begin to explore new ways to conserve water. How much water does it take to flush a toilet? To take a shower? To fill the wading pool? What water uses should be considered essential?

Explore alternate sources of water. How feasible is it to rely on ocean water?

Investigate how pollution affects the water supply and plants and animals confronted with pollution. What happens as the result of an oil spill? If industry dumps hot water into a river?

All children will need to keep a change of clothes at the center. If swimming is available in the area, they will also need their own swimming suits. Check with local health regulations before the excursion.

Discuss how weather affects planning water activities.

IDEAS TO TRY

Float cork, feathers, balsa wood, leaves, small boats.

Blow soap bubbles.

Slip and slide.

Build dams and bridges.

Wash seashells, stones.

Clean fishbowls, aquarium, pet cages.

Water plants, lawn, and garden.

Wash cars.

Wash playhouse furniture, windows; mop playhouse floor.

Make rainbows with oil and water.

Do mud puddle paintings.

Careful conservation of water is now a necessity. Soapy water might be used to wash riding toys, to clean doll clothes, or to scrub the sidewalk.

stone, sponge, or piece of cloth in a measuring cup of water; watch which things mix and which do not mix with water — oil, salt, syrup, sugar, baking soda.

Fill glasses with different amounts of water (color with food coloring if desired) and play melodies.

Encourage children to experiment with sand. When does it pour easily? When can it be molded? What happens if water is poured on it?

Where does sand come from? How can you find out?

What other minerals are extracted from the earth? How are they used?

Fill muffin tin with water. In three of the sections place three basic colors. Children can use eyedroppers to mix colors.

Explore what happens when mud dries. What different kinds of soil create different types of mud?

Measure rainfall.

Select a site for mud play with the children — where should it be? What considerations should be made?

Encourage children to begin a water conservation campaign. Who can they contact? What can they do?

Experiment with water temperature; study water through sunlight; observe reflection in water puddles; observe what happens to water squirted on warm cement; watch air bubbles rise to top of water in a full jar of water; watch what happens when a jar of water covered with a lid is placed outside in winter weather; watch snow melt when brought into a warm room, watch what happens to the waterline when you put a

Sandbox—Five or six tires arranged in a circle can be the basis for an interesting sandbox. The center space and each of the tires can be filled with sand. One tire can be used for water play if cut in half and filled with water.

Waterfalls—Cut milk cartons in half lengthwise. Punch a hole in one side and extend a straw through the hole. Build various levels in the sandbox; arrange the cartons so that the water drops from one carton to the next, forming a waterfall.

Walnut shell boat—Partly fill half a walnut shell with melted wax. When wax is set, pierce a 1″ × ½″ paper sail with a toothpick and stick the toothpick into the wax.

Origami paper boats are fun to fold. What kinds of paper work best?

Soap bubbles
½ cup dish washing liquid
2 tbsp. glycerin
1 gallon water

Balsa wood sailboat	
Balsa wood	Rubber bands
¼″ dowel stick	Saws
Glue	Ruler
Sheets	Tubs for dye
Dye	¼″ brace (drill) and bit

Children cut balsa wood into boat shapes of their own design. With a ¼″ bit, drill a hole into the wooden hull but not through it. Cut a length of dowel stick, taking care not to make it too long. (This raises the boat's center of gravity and it will tip over easier.) Glue dowel into the hole. To make a sail, cut sheets into squares, gather fabric randomly and wrap tightly with rubber bands. Dip sails into tubs of hot fabric dye. After sails have dried, attach to crossbars (Popsicle sticks work well) and attach crossbars to dowel mast with nails.

Resources

Brown, S.E. *Bubbles, Rainbows and Worms.* Mt. Rainier, Maryland: Gryphon House, 1981.

Forte, I., and Frank, M. *Puddles and Wings and Grapevine Swings.* Nashville, Tenn.: Incentive Publication, 1982.

Harris, D. "The Wonderful World of Water Play." *P.T.A. Magazine,* June 1967.

Hill, D.M. *Mud, Sand, and Water.* Washington, D.C.: National Association for the Education of Young Children, 1977.

Schools Council Publications. *Early Experiences.* Milwaukee, Wis.: Macdonald—Raintree, 1980.

Nutrition/Cooking 13

Preparing food—and the menu planning, shopping, setting the table, serving, eating, and cleanup that go with it—gives children wonderful opportunities to use all five senses: to see the beauty of color, shape, and arrangement; to smell everything from apple pie to boiled cabbage; to taste salty, sour, sweet, bitter, bland foods and spices; to touch warm, soft bread dough, slippery fish, rough coconuts; to hear popcorn popping, water boiling, pancakes frying.

At the same time, opportunities for delicious anticipation arise while the cake is baking, the ice cream is freezing, or the gelatin is setting, topped off by the physical pleasure of eating the finished product. Sometimes this pleasure may be increased by opportunities to find a favorite eating spot inside in a box or corner, or outside rooms and yards into more open settings such as parks and recreation areas for picnics. Cooking gives children the opportunity to use what they have learned, to do some of the things adults do, and to turn out products that can be appreciated, admired, eaten, shared, or given as gifts. Cook-ing also gives the child a chance to be away from the larger group, and sometimes to be alone with an adult or child, working almost as if they were at home.

There are opportunities to develop hand-eye coordination in such activities as shelling peas, sorting vegetables, and decorating cookies, as well as opportunities to develop large and small muscles by cranking the ice cream freezer, pushing the shopping cart, rolling dough, mashing potatoes, and sifting the flour. There are opportunities to solve problems and see the effects of attempted solutions—what to do when something sticks to a pan, when the dough does not rise, when liquids are too hot, when something might spoil. There are opportunities to find out more about such things as:

Time—the length of one hour, five minutes, one minute; how long it takes to bake bread or boil an egg.

Changes in matter—gelatin changing to a solid in the refrigerator and liquid in the sun; egg whites expanding and thickening when beaten.

Number—counting change at the market; napkins and cups necessary for lunch or snack; number of eggs, tablespoons of shortening, cups of flour in a recipe; computing cost per serving.

Quantity—measuring cups and pints and quarts, dividing recipes in half, estimating number of servings.

Classification and grouping—carrots, peas, beans are vegetables; water, milk, vanilla extract are liquids.

Cooking gives children many opportunities to read and write as they work with recipes, adapt quantities, and follow directions. It helps them to extend vocabularies by using and naming such objects as graters, strainers, and sieves, and processes such as fold, whip, and simmer. Planning menus, picnics, and parties gives children more opportunities to develop language skills as well as to learn how to work with other children and adults.

Cooking provides the perfect vehicle for helping children learn about nutrition and health. Planning for snacks and meals can be done with the children—selecting dairy products, fresh fruits and vegetables, meats, and whole grains, rather than sweets, processed foods, and items with little or no nutritional value. A garden at the center (see Chapter 14) can be an additional stimulus to interest in fresh produce.

Along with a balanced diet goes the proper care of food—washing fresh fruits and vegetables, refrigerating items which spoil easily, cooking with small amounts of water to preserve vitamins and minerals. A good source of free information on nutrition and preparation is your local cooperative extension service.

By eating foods from many cultures and learning about the traditions that go with them, children can learn about other people, or perhaps share part of their family's world with friends and teachers. They can also learn that different ethnic foods are not bad or strange but can be fun, delicious, and interesting.

Cooking also helps children learn that safety is no accident. Turning pan handles away from the outside of the stove and using pot holders to take things out of the oven are just two safety measures cooks employ.

Cooking offers almost limitless opportunities for learning and sharing.

EQUIPMENT

Bottle opener
Bowls
Cake pans
Can opener
Colander
Cookie cutters
Cookie sheets

Cutting boards
Eggbeater
First aid kit
Fork—long-handled
Grater—hand, four-sided
Knives—paring
Measuring spoons and cups
Pancake turner
Pitchers
Refrigerator
Rolling pin
Saucepans
Scrapers—rubber
Sifter
Skillet—heavy
Spatulas
Spoons—wooden, slotted
Stove
Strainers
Vegetable brushes
Vegetable peeler

Add if possible:

Apple corer
Blender
Candy thermometer
Cheese slicer
Clock or timer
Corn popper
Egg slicer
Electric frying pan
Electric mixer
Gelatin molds
Hot plate—two-burner, adjustable heat
Ice cream freezer
Meat grinder
Muffin tins
Orange juicer—hand squeezing
Pastry brushes
Portable bake oven
Potato masher
Tongs

STORAGE

Labeled boxes, shelves, baskets, and cabinets, nesting materials when possible.
Plastic bags, closed containers.
Knives kept separate from other utensils.
Storage should be located near appliances.

TOPICS TO TALK ABOUT WITH CHILDREN

Sequence of how things are grown, harvested, packaged, transported, placed in stores and markets, sold, transported to homes, cooked, served.

The nutritional value of different foods, and why good nutrition is vital to health.

Preparation of foods—washing, cooking, serving.

Foods which can be eaten raw—spinach, lettuce, fruits—but can also be used in a variety of different ways—creamed spinach, lettuce in salads, fruits in gelatin, pies, cookies, or cakes.

Safety factors—turning pot handles back from the front of the stove, mopping up spills immediately, cutting safely away from body, using pot holders, not bending faces over steaming pots, using a cutting board.

Changes which take place when foods are chilled or heated—gelatin, popcorn, rice, macaroni, split peas.

The difference in the taste and texture of different foods—sweet orange, sour lemon, soft bread, crunchy toast, spicy enchiladas, mild tapioca pudding.

- Names, colors, and textures of different foods—apples, cucumbers, peppers, bananas, green beans, peas, squash.
- The economics of purchasing food in markets, neighborhood stores, delicatessens, roadside stands.
- How to determine quality, quantity, weight, size, price.
- The people who grow, process, package, and sell foods.
- Holiday and ethnic foods.
- Preparing and serving well-balanced meals.
- Indoor and outdoor cooking.
- Formulate plans with children for shopping, preparation, serving, and cleanup. Discuss how weather affects food supplies. What role does agriculture play in the economy?
- Alternatives to traditional food and nutritional food sources.

IDEAS TO TRY

- Take trips to a neighborhood market, fish market, bakery, delicatessen, vegetable farm, orchard, cannery, dairy, meat processing plant. Discuss and record children's experiences.
- Children can plan menus, prepare shopping lists, and shop. Encourage parents to include children in these activities at home.
- Use mechanical equipment—eggbeater, ice cream freezer, blender, scale, electric frying pan, portable bake oven, corn popper. Discuss what makes them work.
- Shell peas, prepare green beans, scrape carrots, squeeze lemons and oranges for juice.
- Shake containers of cream to make butter, add salt or eat on saltines.
- Make gelatin, applesauce, vegetable soup.
- Bake bread, biscuits, muffins, popovers, gingerbread people, yeast bread and rolls, pizza.
- Toast sandwiches, make cinnamon toast, fry pancakes and potatoes.
- Make sandwiches for a picnic lunch.
- Pop corn, grate coconut, shred lettuce.
- Blend milk and juices for milkshakes.
- Roast hot dogs, ears of corn, potatoes, hamburgers, kabobs on sticks, bread and buns over charcoal; toast marshmallows.
- Plan snacks around different cultures.
- Make desserts—ice cream, puddings, cakes, cookies, pies, custards.
- Plan and prepare snacks—stuff celery; cut up cauliflower, beets, and turnips; serve different shaped crackers and sandwiches.
- Children can write a cookbook or prepare a recipe file including favorite recipes as well as those continually used. Include parents' favorites.
- Devil, hard boil, fry, scramble, and poach eggs.

Snack ideas for children to prepare

Ants on a log (recipe p. 68)
Apple wedges
Applesauce (recipe p. 68)
Bananas—sliced or frozen
Bean sprout sandwiches
Bread (recipe p. 68)
Cabbage leaves
Carrot sticks
Carrot sticks with olives on ends
Celery sticks—stuffed with cream cheese or peanut butter
Cheese with pretzels or crackers
Cinnamon toast—painted (recipe p. 68)
Cookies; paintbrush cookies (recipe p. 68)
Crackers—assorted, spread with cream cheese or peanut butter
Cupcake ice cream cones (recipe p. 68)
Cupcakes—decorated
Donuts—easy (recipe p. 69)
Frozen fruit treats (recipe p. 68)
Fruit gelatin
Funnel cakes (recipe p. 68)
Granola—homemade
Green pepper slices
Ice cream
Melon chunks
Muffins
Nuts—assorted
Orange wedges
Peanut butter balls (recipe p. 68)
Pigs in blankets (recipe p. 68)
Popcorn
Pretzels (recipe p. 69)
Puddings
Pudding-wiches (recipe p. 68)
Pumpkin seeds—baked
Stone soup (recipe p. 69)
Toast—spread with peanut butter, cheese, or honey
Tomato wedges

Applesauce

Cut apples in quarters, leaving skins on. Add ½″ of water to pot; bring to boil. Cover and cook slowly for 20–30 minutes or until soft. Add sugar if needed. Force through sieve. Serve warm or cold. (Changes in color, texture, and form which are vividly demonstrated in this procedure are a delight for children to observe.)

Frozen fruit treats

Squeeze enough juice to fill ice cube tray. Add sugar or honey if needed. When partially frozen, insert stick upright into each section of tray and let freeze.

Peanut butter balls

½ cup peanut butter	Raisins
2 cups powdered milk	Whole grain cereal
2 tablespoons honey	Coconut

Mix peanut butter, powdered milk, and honey. Add raisins if desired. Roll in balls, then roll balls in cereal or coconut. Chill.

Pigs in blankets

| Bread slices | Cheese slices |
| Hot dogs | Toothpicks |

Place cheese and hot dog on bread. Roll two ends of bread up around hot dog and secure with toothpick. Bake in preheated oven until hot (350°F for 20 minutes).

Bread

1 cup lukewarm water	2 tablespoons sugar
1 cake of yeast	2 cups flour
2 tablespoons shortening	1 teaspoon salt

Add yeast to water and stir until yeast melts. Add shortening and sugar; stir. Then add flour. Be sure dough is very stiff. Set in warm place until dough doubles in size (about 1 hour). Add salt. Shape into 8 rolls; set in warm place until rolls double in size again (about 1 hour). Bake about 15 minutes at 450° F (230° C).

Painted cinnamon toast

Bread	Cinnamon
Milk	Sugar
Food coloring	Butter

Mix "paint" by combining food coloring with milk. Paint designs or pictures on one side of the bread with small clean paintbrushes. Place bread, painted side up, under broiler and toast. While bread is still hot, spread with butter and sprinkle with cinnamon and sugar.

Pudding-wiches

1½ cups milk	1 package instant pudding, any flavor
½ cup peanut butter	
	24 graham crackers

Add milk slowly to peanut butter in a deep, narrow bottom bowl. Blend until smooth. Add pudding mix; beat slowly until well mixed (about 2 minutes). Let stand 5 minutes. Spread filling about ½″ thick on 12 graham crackers; top with remaining crackers. Freeze until firm (about 3 hours). Makes 12.

Paintbrush cookies

Sugar cookie dough   Egg yolk paint

Roll out any recipe of sugar cookie dough. Cut out designs and place on a greased cookie sheet. With small, clean paintbrushes, draw designs with egg yolk paint.

Egg yolk paint — Blend one egg yolk with ¼ teaspoon water. Divide into 2 or 3 small cups and add a different food coloring to each cup.

Ants on a log

| Celery | Raisins |
| Peanut butter | |

Separate and wash celery stalks. Fill each stalk with peanut butter. Place raisins in a row on top of the peanut butter.

Cupcake ice cream cones

Cake batter   Cup-style ice cream cones

Mix cake batter according to directions. Pour into ice cream cones until ¾ full. Bake according to directions for cupcakes. A scoop of ice cream on top makes this an extra special treat for parties.

Funnel cakes

| Pancake batter | Syrup |
| Butter | |

After mixing the pancake batter, fill meat basters with the batter or pour it through a funnel onto a hot griddle, making shapes, letters, or designs. Cook as any pancake.

Easy donuts

Refrigerator-style baking powder biscuits
Cooking oil

Powdered sugar, cinnamon sugar, or chocolate

Mold each biscuit into any shape desired. Drop the molded donut into hot fat and fry until golden and puffy. Roll the donut in powdered sugar, cinnamon sugar, or chocolate, and eat.

Pretzels

1 package active dry yeast
⅛ cup of hot water
1⅓ cups warm water

¼ cup brown sugar
5 cups flour
coarse kosher salt

Add yeast to hot water and stir until yeast dissolves. Add warm water and brown sugar. Add flour to mixture and stir until it is smooth and does not stick to sides of bowl. Put on floured board and knead until stretchy and smooth. Roll dough into a rope 12–14 inches long. Pinch off pieces and bend into a U shape. Cross one end over the other end. Place on a greased and salted cookie sheet and bake for 8 minutes in a 475° F oven.

Stone soup

7 cups water
4 large carrots
3 onions
4 beef boullion cubes
4 large potatoes

4 stalks celery
1 can tomatoes
1 tsp. salt
1 scrubbed large grey stone

Wash and chop vegetables. Put stone in large pot. Add water and the chopped vegetables. Cook until the vegetables are tender.

Cooking aprons

Children can make their own aprons from windowshade material or lightweight oilcloth. Fabric should be folded in half and pattern marked to fit the child. Cut with pinking shears. If desired, edges can be turned and stitched. Use colorful yarn to tie at the waist.

Cook's Apron

Resources

Cooking and Eating with Children—A Way to Learn. Washington, D.C.: Association for Childhood Education International, 1974.

Fun and Learning With Foods. Nutrition and Child Development, Inc., P.O. Box 4568, Casper, Wyoming 82604.

Stein, S. *The Kids' Kitchen Takeover.* New York: Workman, 1975.

Super Snacks. School Ages NOTES, P.O. Box 120674, Nashville, Tenn. 37212.

Veitch, B., and Harms, T. *Cook and Learn.* Menlo Park, Calif.: Addison-Wesley, 1981.

Wanamaker, N.; Hearn, K.; and Richarz, S. *More Than Graham Crackers: Nutrition Education and Food Preparation and Young Children.* Washington, D.C.: National Association for the Education of Young Children, 1979.

Waxter, J. *The Science Cookbook.* Belmont, Calif.: David S. Lake, 1981.

Observing, experimenting, checking in books, and asking adults, children can find answers to many of the questions they have about their surroundings.

Science, Nature, and Gardening

14

Children love to learn about the world—light, heat, sound, electricity, animals, plants, earth, space. *Things happen!* Seeds come up, magnets attract, snow falls, water freezes. Observing, experimenting, checking in books, and asking adults, children can find answers to many of the questions they have about their surroundings: Do earthworms have teeth? How do plants absorb water? What is sound? How does a switch turn the light on? Children can also make things happen themselves. For example, they can make an electric current flow when they complete the circuit between a battery and a light.

Children discover many of the basic principles of physics and chemistry by watching what happens as they do various things. They can learn about:

- *Force*—by pushing boxes and pulling wagons.
- *Forms of energy* (and the idea of energy as a force that does work)—by watching as steam makes the teakettle whistle, gasoline makes the car run, sun and water make plants grow, food makes people feel strong, electricity makes the record player run.
- *Sound*—by feeling vibrations on a drum, seeing the vibrations of a tuning fork, twanging a rubber band guitar.
- *Magnetism*—by using magnets to pick up steel or iron but not aluminum, plastic, or wood; by watching two magnets attract or repel each other.
- *Friction*—by seeing roller skates make sparks on bumpy pavement, feeling wood get hot while sandpapering it.
- *Acceleration*—by rolling slowly down from the top of the hill and really whirling by the time they get to the bottom.
- *Chemical reactions* (or lack of them)—by mixing baking soda and vinegar to make a miniature volcano, shaking oil and water together.

Working with seeds, plants, batteries, animals, and insects helps children to look at things carefully and to notice their shape, color, size, weight, texture, action, and behavior. Children learn to think of one experience or discovery *in relationship to another*—"This moth has six legs like the butterfly"; "It rained the last time we had clouds like this, too"—and to notice similarities, differences, and changes. They begin to speculate, plan experiments, and draw conclusions as they grow older.

By making an ant farm like the one in a book they have read, displaying rocks or insects the way the museum did, trying out a suggestion that levers can move heavy objects, children can discover that what they learned from reading or going on field trips or talking in class can be useful and practical and lead to original exploration. Working with adults who encourage curiosity, children can learn to feel comfortable asking questions and saying, "I don't know," "I don't understand yet," and "How can I find out?" They can learn to figure out their own answers to questions and problems by observing, testing, checking, and reaching conclusions.

Children can become aware of their own growth as they discover they need longer pants legs and sweater sleeves and bigger shoes. They can observe the orderly sequence of life stages—conception, birth, growth, old age, death—repeated over and over again as the hamsters mate and baby hamsters are born, polliwogs grow into frogs, the aged rabbit dies. This helps them see themselves as part of the overall pattern of the world of living things.

By seeing tiny bugs hiding in grass and under rocks, bees pollinating flowers, rain and sun nourishing plants, large insects eating smaller ones, birds eating insects, animals eating birds—and then considering their own use of trees, water, air, and animals, children can develop a sense of how living and nonliving things depend on each other. They can learn to respect the world of nature and from this respect will grow the desire to learn to protect it as well as enjoy it.

Children can also learn to work together—to use a common bottle to put bugs in, to share the bells and light and wires for the gadget board, to take turns feeding the turtle, to plan together to complete a project. They have opportunities to learn words related to their observations and discoveries—erosion, pollination, mutation, adaptability, conservation, pollution, fertilization, reflection, vibration—which accurately tell what they found out.

Children have opportunities to read and write, pursuing a topic in a science book, writing notebooks about weather, labeling bottles with specimens, writing up a project, making up lists of materials and equipment needed, making signs asking that others not touch their project. They find these skills useful ways for discovering, recording, and communicating. Children also have opportunities to learn how to use equipment such as microscopes, prisms, magnifying glasses, tape recorders, and record players carefully and correctly. They learn to accept the responsibilities of caring for the equipment, animals, gardens, and individual projects.

EQUIPMENT

Aprons
Balance
Binoculars
Camera
Compass
Electric bells
Flashlight
Funnels
Gardening tools
Globe
Gyroscope
Kaleidoscope
Kites
Magnets—various sizes and shapes
Magnifying glass
Maps
Microscope
Mirrors
Musical instruments
Pails
Prisms
Reference books
Scale
Stand magnifier
Stethoscope
Telescope/periscope
Thermometer
Timer
Tire pump
Tongs
Tuning fork

MATERIALS

Adhesive tape
Ant farm
Aquarium
Balloons
Balsa wood
Batteries—dry cell
Birdfeeders
Bird nests
Bulbs, seeds, plants
Cages for classroom pets
Cardboard, cardboard tubes
Cellophane paper
Cork
Crepe paper
Feathers
Felt pens
Fish, toads, frogs, tadpoles
Hardware for gadget boards
Iron filings
Jars, cans, boxes, and milk cartons
Masking tape
Nails, screws
Notebooks
Pinwheels
Plaster of Paris
Plunger and other suction gadgets
Rocks, pebbles
Rubber bands
Rubber tubing—pieces
Ruler, tape measure
Salt—coarse
Sand
Sandpaper
Scissors
Seashells
Soda, starch, sugar, salt, vinegar
Soil
Straws
Syringes, squeeze bottles

Terrarium
Vivarium for toads and frogs
Yardstick

STORAGE

Boxes, cabinets, shelves, baskets, hooks—label or draw sketches where equipment or material goes.

Special containers for breakable items (as few as possible).

Plastic bags for small articles.

Several small cabinets rather than one large one so children have easy access to materials.

Locked cupboards with containers clearly labeled for chemicals such as alcohol, turpentine, iodine, bleach, glycerine, etc.

TOPICS TO TALK ABOUT WITH CHILDREN

Machines with wheels which help us get from place to place—taxis, bicycles, buses, automobiles, trains, airplanes, motorcycles, wheelchairs.

Other things with wheels which are fun—roller skates, skateboards, merry-go-round, Ferris wheel, scooter, wagon, record player, fishing reel.

Items with wheels which help us in the house and garden—lawn mower, casters on furniture, telephone dial, eggbeater, wheelbarrow.

Magnets—what they attract and what they do not attract; a magnet attracts through paper, glass, and wood; how magnets function as compasses.

How vacuum cleaners, blenders, hair dryers, irons, and various other electrical equipment—lamps, refrigerators, waffle irons, percolators, clocks, television sets, hot plates, streetlights, traffic signals—work.

How wall plugs, light sockets, extension cords, and light switches are used.

Energy—food is a source of energy; light energy helps us find our way; wind or water produces electrical energy.

The need for conserving limited fuel resources.

Things which help us in our daily living—typewriters, can openers, computers.

How things look through a magnifying glass, a telescope, a periscope, binoculars.

How to use and store garden tools; safety measures.

Composition, color, and texture of soil; different colors of soil—red, black, brown, yellow; different textures—sandy, rocky, hard, soft, clay.

Seeds—soaking before planting; putting bulbs in refrigerator before planting; how seeds travel—wind, birds, fur of animals, clothing, spontaneous shoot out; time to plant seeds and bulbs; the effect of sun, light, and temperature on germination, soil moisture, grafting.

Preparation of garden soil—dug, spaded, fertilized; why clods of soil are broken before planting.

Grasses of importance—rice, corn, wheat, rye, barley, oats; where they grow; how seeds are sown; how crops are used.

Plants—parts of plants and their functions. Plants are living things which grow and reproduce; different kinds of plants live in different environments—some, such as the cactus, require sunlight, others, such as the fern, prefer shade.

Weather—temperature, wind, and humidity. How weather affects our lives.

Children can learn to respect the world of nature, and from this respect will grow the desire to learn to protect it as well as enjoy it.

What can be eaten raw and what must be cooked.

How animals and plants depend on each other.

Concept of shelters—practical aspects such as use, need, strength, beauty. Discuss structures created by man—condos, apartments, houses, castles, pyramids. Follow up with building projects.

Value of insects, bugs, and spiders, earthworms, snails—how they look and move, what they do, what gardeners should know about them.

Space—how rockets are propelled into space; one's relationship to space.

Household chemicals and how they are used —vinegar, salt, sugar, ammonia, baking soda, washing soda, detergent, vegetable dyes, bleaches.

IDEAS TO TRY

Plant an outdoor garden. Prepare the earth, marking seeded areas with signs of what is being grown. Water, weed, harvest, taste, discuss.

Grow carrot, turnip, beet tops, potato, and pineapple in dish of water.

Sprinkle flax, parsley, or bird seed on top of damp sponge placed in a pie pan.

Fill a tray with damp cotton. Put in rows of beet, radish, bean, and lettuce seeds. Keep moist, transplant.

Plant bulbs in small cartons, cans, or paper cups which can be given as gifts.

Grow herbs in an indoor garden. Study seed catalogs for a wide selection.

Collect seed pods. Paint, arrange, and string.

Arrange flowers. Learn their names. Learn functions of pistil, stamen, anther, nectar, blossom, petal, bud.

Make an indoor observation shelf and study the effects of the lack of air, sun, and/or water on plant growth.

Take nature walks and record what was seen and heard. Take care to leave the area just as it was found or better.

Bring in samples of the different types of structures that animals build—bird nests, honey combs—and pictures of spider webs, tunnels plowed by gophers, termite towers, and so forth.

Grow a fast-growing plant, and every three or four days make a strip of paper the height of the plant. Glue the strips on a piece of paper in sequence for a record of the growth of the plant.

Make leaf prints on paper, cardboard, or plaster of Paris.

Make a leaf collection. Note similarities and differences in shape, size, color, texture, thickness of leaves. Learn the names of the trees from which the leaves came.

Put some soil in a jar and cover it tightly. Why do drops of moisture gather in the jar?

Press flowers; make wax paper flower and leaf transparencies.

Collect nails, clips, thumbtacks, wire, seeds, buttons, etc., and see which are attracted to magnets.

Make a museum of rocks, shells, nuts, insects, nests, plants, bark, stones, cacti.

Collect different types of rock—pumice, quartz, limestone with shells, mica, coal, lava, rocks with plant imprints.

Make gadget boards with lights, switches, bells, and batteries.

Collect bells and note differences in sounds.

Play tuning fork or other instruments which make sounds when struck.

Fill glasses with different amounts of water (color with food coloring) and note differences in sounds when struck.

Experiment with matter—bulk, weight, divisibility, porosity, elasticity, impenetrability—by noting differences in size and weight of blocks; weight of child on a scale; sawing wood into two pieces or cutting fruit in half; wiping up spilled milk with a sponge; pouring water into a sandbox; popping corn; cooking rice; stretching rubber bands; trying to hammer nails into very hard wood.

Experiment with measurements—length or height using rulers, tape measures, and yardsticks; volume using cups, pitchers, or other containers for milk or juice; time using a calendar, three-minute glass timer, or clock; weight using a scale; temperature using a thermometer.

Make "Rube Goldberg" machines from odds and ends, pulleys, gears, clocks and watches, objects with wheels, and wind-up toys.

Care for, feed, and observe frogs, toads, tadpoles, horned toads, lizards, salamanders, rabbits, guinea pigs, gerbils, hamsters.

Put snails in a jar with air holes in the lid and observe with a magnifying glass.

Make a worm farm using a box or tray filled with soil; add a litle cornmeal and keep moist.

Make an ant village in a tray filled with anthill soil, small piece of moist sponge, and sugar; place tray in pan of water.

Fill a jar with seawater; put in some seaweed. Cap tightly so air does not get in and seaweed will last for months if set near light. Shake occasionally so the seaweed moves.

Incubate eggs. Observe and care for baby chicks. Be sure you have provision for care of chickens as they grow.

Observe shadows; make shadows. Notice the difference in length of a shadow according to the time of day.

Use air pump to blow up balloons; make paper airplanes; use walnut shell boats (see p. 63) with sails and blow around in a shallow pan.

Collect pictures and make scrapbooks; for example, make a scrapbook of appliances which use electricity—vacuum cleaners, irons, electric stoves, toasters, mixers, blenders, shavers, hot plates, hair dryers, lamps, lawn mowers.

Gardening projects

Friendly egghead—Hard boil an egg; carefully cut off top and hollow out the edible portion and eat. Use a felt pen to draw a design or face on the bottom half of the shell. Staple a strip of stiff paper together to make a supporting base. Fill eggshell with potting soil, then plant grass seed. Keep soil moist.

Potato farming—Put soil into an opaque plastic trash bag until it is almost full. Select a sprouted potato and cut into pieces, making sure that two or more sprouts are in each section. Plant three cuttings in a bag, setting each five inches deep. Leave sack open at the top. Put in a warm, sunny place and keep the soil moist but not soggy. When leaf growth is four or five inches high, save the biggest plant and discard the others. After five or six weeks, gently reach into the soil to see if you can feel the new potatoes.

Sprouts—Buy alfalfa seeds at a health food store—one ounce will yield four or five crops of sprouts. Use two tablespoons for each quart jar you start. Soak seeds overnight; drain well and put in jar. Stretch a piece of cheesecloth over the jar and secure with a rubber band. Set the jar in a warm spot in indirect light. Rinse seeds with water twice a day; drain well after each rinsing. The seeds will sprout in four or five days. Use the sprouts in salads or in sandwiches.

Wooden birdfeeders or houses—Children may wish to construct wooden birdfeeders or houses. Prior to construction, adults may wish to initiate discussions about birds native to the area and their eating habits; set up a library center with materials about birds as well as methods for observation and identification, including illustrations of birds; encourage children to keep individual observation logs including information on birds sighted (identifiable traits—wings, color, feathers, beaks), choice of feeders, frequency of sightings, time of day, etc. The information can be charted to share with other children.

Children can plan and take trips to various places as they extend their knowledge of science—farms, factories, zoos, ponds, arboretums, botanical gardens, nurseries, museums, airports, etc.

Explore careers in science with children. Help them discover occupations which may be new to them—forester, fisheries and wildlife management, medical researcher, food chemist, engineer, etc.

Stimulate new and creative ways of thinking about the world—how different it will be when the children have grown up!

SOME "AROUND THE SCHOOL YARD" ACTIVITIES*

Using the senses

EQUIPMENT NEEDED:

1 sheet of drawing paper (8½ × 11") (manila) per child.

Each child brings one dark crayon (green, black, brown, etc.)

Each adult leader should have a clip-board and paper and pencil.

List as many of the children's comments as possible for each activity.

Tell the children you are writing down their descriptions. At intervals throughout the activity, read back their comments to them.

At the end of each activity, read what was said as a summary. Group leaders should give the comments and descriptions to the teachers at the end of the field trip for use back at school to make experience charts and story-writing.

"Sound" Hike — (10–15 minutes)

Group leader takes kids for walk.

Stop at intervals along the way. Have kids close eyes and listen for 30 seconds. At end of 30 seconds, kids describe a sound they heard.

Group leader should write down the way each kid described his sound.

---

* From the *Investigating Your Environment series*, U.S. Forest Service, San Francisco, CA.

Try to stop in different places so there will be a variety of sounds to be heard.

See how many different sounds your group can discover.

Ask:

Which sound did you like best?
Why?
Does it remind you of something else?
Which sound is the loudest? The quietest?
The highest? The lowest?

Mini-Forest (Investigating an Arm-Circle of Grass) — (Approximately 15 minutes)

1. Lie on the ground, face down.
2. Make a circle by stretching your arms out in front of you on the ground.
3. Find at least five different plants inside that circle made with your arms.
4. See if you can find any tiny animals crawling through the grass.
5. What else do you see? (Any dead leaves or twigs?)
6. Spread the grass apart and describe what you see.

Big Idea — Many plants and animals live together in a community.

"Touch and Feel" Hike — (Approximately 10–15 minutes)

Group leader takes kids for a walk. Gives following directions at intervals along the walk. (Add others when appropriate).

1. Find the *hairiest* leaf around. Bring back a tiny bit of it. Compare with your other group members.
2. Find the *softest* leaf.
3. Find the *smoothest* rock.

4. Find the *roughest* twig.
5. Find something *cool*.
6. Find something *warm*.
7. Find something *bumpy*.
8. Find something *dry*.

"Color" Hike

1. Look for things that are different colors of green. Bring back 3 or 4 green things. Arrange them in your hand according to lightest green to darkest green.
2. Find and describe things that are: yellow — pink — brown — grey.

Math measurement

Determine length of step. Use this unit of measurement to:

1. Calculate perimeters and areas of schoolyard activity spaces (playfield, ball diamonds, open fields, etc.). Convert measurements to yards, meters.
2. Construct a conversion scale for metric measurements using the length of your step.
3. Find out how many times you need to run around the playfield to run a mile.
4. Find out how many acres are on your playfield.

Things to do with trees

Observe and compare the shapes of trees.
How many shapes can you find?
Discuss the shapes. Is it triangular? Like a column? Evenly tapered? Low and spreading? Regular? Irregular?
Find two trees with distinctly different shapes and sketch them.
Look for different shapes of trees on the horizon.

Weed patches

1. Look for the different colors of the plants. Arrange the colors in a list—lightest to darkest:

   _____ _____

   _____ _____

   _____ _____

2. Count and record the different kinds of plants that are below your knees: _____

   a. How many plants have few leaves? _____

   b. How many plants have many leaves? _____

   c. How many kinds of plants are stickery? _

   d. Do any of the plants have flowers? _____

      List the colors of the flowers:

   _____

   e. Do any of the plants have seed pods? _____

      Describe the different pods: _____

   _____

3. Are there any plants higher than your head?

   _____

   Are there many, or just a few? _____

   Describe these plants: _____

   _____

On a separate piece of paper, choose one of the following to do:

a. Choose one weed and write a riddle about it, using four of the five senses to describe it. Which of our five senses would you not use? _____

b. Write a poem describing the weed, or a poem telling about the color "green."

c. Write an imaginary story explaining how the tallest weed became so tall.

Resources

Caney, S. *Invention Book*. New York: Workman, 1985.

Cobb, V. *Science Experiments You Can Eat*. Philadelphia: Lippincott, 1972.

Early (Science) Experiences. Milwaukee, Wis.: Macdonald Educational, 1980.

Forte, I. *Nature Crafts*. Nashville, Tenn.: Incentive Publications, 1985.

Gardner, R. *Science Around the House*. New York: Julian Messner, 1985.

Habben, D. *Science Experiments That Really Work*. Chicago: Follet, 1970.

Herbert, D. *Mr. Wizard's Supermarket Science*. New York: Random House, 1980.

Holt, B. *Science With Young Children*. Washington, D.C.: National Association for the Education of Young Children, 1977.

Hucklesby, S. *Opening Up the Classroom: A Walk Around the School*. Urbana, Ill.: ERIC/EECE, 1971.

Katz, A. *Nature Watch: Exploring Nature With Your Children*. Menlo Park, Calif.: Addison-Wesley, 1986.

Knight, M.E., and Graham, T.L. *Rainbows*. Atlanta, Ga.: Humanics Limited, 1986.

Koehler, C., and Koehler, A. *Indoor and Outdoor Gardening for Young People*. New York: Grosset and Dunlap, 1977.

McIntyre, M., ed. *Early Childhood and Science*. Washington, D.C.: National Science Teachers Association, 1984.

Mitchell, J. *The Curious Naturalist*. Englewood Cliffs, N.J.: Prentice-Hall, 1980.

Sisson, E.A. *Nature With Children of All Ages*. Englewood Cliffs, N.J.: Prentice-Hall, 1982.

Stein, S. *The Science Book*. New York: Workman, 1979.

Wyler, R. *Science Fun With Peanuts and Popcorn*. New York: Julian Messner, 1986.

Wyler, R. *Science Fun With Toy Boats and Planes*. New York: Julian Messner, 1986.

Parents and Staff: A Partnership

15

Parents and staff have something very important in common—the children. Every good program puts the needs of the children first, but takes into consideration the needs of the parents and staff as well. Generally what benefits the children benefits the parents and staff. A high-quality program's philosophy and goals evolve from these intertwined needs and should be included in general information available to prospective parents.

PARENTS

Meeting the developmental needs of each child is not always easy, particularly in a school-age program serving many children of different ages. The children themselves are often the best guide. Look closely at the kindergartners' use of the block area, for example, and compare that with what you see the 8-year-olds construct in the same area with the same blocks.

A parallel principle applies to parents' needs. Observe and listen closely to what they say and do. Above all, they need validation for and understanding of the complicated lives they lead. When you ask them to participate in your program, be sure the activity is well-planned and confirms that they are an integral part of your program. To be really helpful to you, parents must know what your program is all about.

Program Description

In addition to their knowledge about program goals and philosophy, parents should know what goes on during the day. Parents usually see a program at the beginning of the day before activities are really under way and just before closing when everything has been put away. Make sure you give each parent a schedule and a copy of the planned activities including free time and "seasonal events."

If you have never put such a description together, take the different activity areas in this book, choose the ones that are appropriate for your program, and assemble a paragraph or two about each one on a sheet of paper. Your parents will have a good idea from this about why each activity area is chosen and how it is responsive to individual children's needs. Make an effort to have the room environment reflect some of the day's fun and learning. (Children love to see their work displayed, too!)

Always keep in mind that different parents have different expectations. Try to listen to the unasked questions about the program and provide each parent with what she or he most wants to know.

Quality Relationships

A central goal for all who work with children in quality programs is strengthening and reinforcing healthy parent-child relationships. All too often staff members view parents as adversaries and blame them for children's difficulties. Little of a constructive nature will be gained from taking this approach. Every good program needs good parent relationships, which benefit the children, the program, and the parents.

Involving Parents

Enlisting parents as partners at the top level —policymaking—contributes a good deal to strong parent-program relationships. Establishing a parent advisory group can be a first step. One of the easiest ways to establish a group is to ask for volunteers. When a few parents have volunteered, hold a short meeting, perhaps a half-hour before closing time, to last no more than an hour. Simple refreshments should be provided. A staff person should stay to provide child care while the group meets (this should be provided for every parent meeting). Prepare an agenda that includes time for sharing concerns about areas both staff and parents agree should be covered.

The first task for this group is to develop a written policy statement for the program. These common concerns are a starting point. Use your discretion as to how many meetings are necessary to develop together a draft policy statement. With busy schedules, it can take a whole school year to develop a statement covering items such as parent volunteer requirements, fee schedules, late pickup, and sick child policies. Once the policy is approved by the parent advisory committee, write a paragraph explaining how and by whom it was developed. Distribute the statement to all the parents. Each should be asked to acknowledge approval by signing it. Return the signed page to the program files.

Remember to distribute the policy to each incoming parent once each year, perhaps in the fall if your program follows the school calendar.

80   A key part of the policy could be a family's agreement to contribute a number of volunteer hours a year. Try to pick a realistic number of hours, such as 10, so that even very busy parents will have a chance of completing the requisite number of hours. Make sure there are a variety of ways to contribute hours, from attending meetings and covering duties so that staff may attend staff meetings, to fixing up or adding to program facilities. Encourage parents to share their individual expertise, or interests and hobbies. A parent who can help the children learn yoga or carpentry or other skills is sure to enhance any program.

Another way to involve parents is to hold a parent meeting, preferably at the beginning of the school year, when there is the largest number of new parents. Make sure reminders are posted both the day before and the day of the meeting; again, provide light refreshments and child care. Try to limit this first meeting to an hour by arranging for the child care to last only an hour. Have the children return to the meeting at that time.

At this first meeting, in addition to an agenda covering the program's philosophy and goals as well as safety and parent concerns, it may be a good idea to distribute a short questionnaire something like the Parent Interest Questionnaire on page 81.

Much useful information may be efficiently collected in this way and future parent meetings may be scheduled according to the parents' wishes.

This initial meeting is an excellent time to deal with such basic issues as safety after dark and homework. These issues invariably come up, and it is preferable for the program staff to take the initiative. Safety issues are apt to be clear cut, but the question of homework is a thorny one. School-age programs should not function as study halls. Children differ as to the amount of time they need to unwind from the pressures of the school day before they must tackle homework. Children differ in *how* they unwind, as well.

One of the best solutions to the homework problem is to put up a chart on the wall in an area that can be used for a quiet time in the room. Those parents who wish their children to do homework may sign up on the chart. The children should sign their names as well. Set aside a half-hour in the afternoon for this quiet time. See if the area can be made more attractive with special pencils, paper, and erasers, and a "homework area" sign. Make sure that any children who are inside at that time are engaged in a quiet activity and that the quiet area stays quiet even after the half-hour is up.

If a questionnaire is used, it is important to be responsive to the parents' requests. "How To Help Your Child in School" is a sure-fire topic for getting parent meetings off to a good start. School district personnel will be more than happy to help you put on such a presentation. Other topics may come up during the year that were not on the questionnaire. Try to be responsive to these, as well.

Although no one wishes to overburden parents with paperwork, have them come in at least once a year to fill out emergency cards and permission slips of the kind necessary for your program. At this time, they should also sign the policy statement you have developed.

PARENT INTEREST QUESTIONNAIRE

Parents are special people. We'd like to get to know you better and plan activities at the program for you and your family. We also need your help with activities and projects. Will you share your ideas and interests by answering the following questions?

Are you interested in meetings to get to know other parents and to learn more about children and the program?

YES   NO   (Circle)

How many meetings would you prefer to have this year?

1   2   3   4   5   6   more   (Circle)

What day of the week is most convenient for your family?

Monday   Tuesday   Wednesday   Thursday   Friday   (Circle)

Would you find afternoon or evening meetings to be more convenient? _____

Would you need transportation to the meetings?

YES   NO   (Circle)

Check the type(s) of meetings you would like:

_____ Intensive study sessions on a specific topic to meet several times over a 4–6 week period.

_____ Several group meetings scheduled throughout the year.

_____ Afternoon coffee and informal discussion sessions.

What topics would be of interest for meetings/discussion sessions? (Check)

_____ Understanding the _____ year old.

_____ Discipline

_____ Books for young children

_____ How to help your child in school

_____ What your child learns in school

_____ Using TV with your child

_____ Other _____

Would you be interested in other types of activities? (Check)

_____ Picnics for parents and child

_____ Field trips for parents and child

_____ Other social events

Would you be interested in participating in "rap sessions" with our family counselor?   YES   NO   (Circle)

You have many skills and interests that we need for our program. Check those activities you enjoy doing.

_____ Cooking

_____ Sewing and mending

_____ Repairing and constructing toys and play equipment

_____ Painting toys and play equipment

_____ Gardening

_____ Visiting other parents

_____ Providing transportation

_____

_____

_____

_____

81

One of the best times to involve parents is around holidays. Try to plan a workshop where parents and children can make presents or decorations together, for example. Working on projects together is an experience that is all too rare for parents and children in this day and age; it can be a great deal of fun as well as a learning experience for all. Potluck suppers are equally fun and a good way for parents and children in the group to get to know one another a little better. Potluck suppers are good to have in conjunction with fund-raising activities, and parents can be really helpful to you in raising funds. Tap them for all their expertise in this area!

Parents as Advocates

Finally, parents can be most helpful as advocates for your program, no matter what your funding source is. Staff, too, can be helpful in this area, but parents make much more effective advocates, particularly with state legislators. To advocate effectively, however, parents need to be fully informed about your program. The need for parent advocacy is a fact of life today. There is no reason to expect the situation to change in the near future.

In Summary

It is important for staff to support the bond between parent and child by including parents in program planning, by inviting parents to participate in as many activities as their schedules allow, and by sharing their special knowledge of children in frequent and supportive conferences and group discussions.

Parents can learn in this nondirective way as they see staff handle problems similar to those they deal with at home. That is why centers should be open to parents. Parents and child care personnel can become mutually supportive, both enriching and enhancing the quality of life for the children.

*   *   *

STAFF

Let's turn now to the other half of the partnership. The quality of your staff in large part determines the quality of your program. For example, any or all of the activities described in this book can be enriching and interesting in a school-age program; each has been tested and evaluated for children of this age. But each could also be irrelevant, uninteresting, or a waste of time without the staff's understanding of each child, an understanding central to the staff member's ability to function well in the program.

Meetings

As part of this process, it is crucial to hold regular, frequent, and searching staff meetings during which adults who interact with the children will exchange information, make interpretations, and attempt to understand the whys and hows of the behaviors they have observed in the children for whom they are responsible.

A weekly staff meeting should be designed to exchange ideas and plans about the program, materials, and activities, and to evaluate completed or continuing aspects of the program. In addition, there should be observations and information exchanged about individual children and significant events and developments in their lives. In any program where several adults interact with one or more children, it is important not only that they pool their perceptions, but that they agree on what ways of interacting will most enrich the child's well-being and development.

Sometimes brief daily exchanges can be extremely helpful. Less formal than a staff meeting, but still professional in their focus on growth and development of children and families, such exchanges may involve a teacher and an aide or the whole program staff. They may last 5 minutes or 15 and must be designed to make the next day at the program pleasant and productive for everyone. When necessary, staff may take over one another's tasks to free individuals for appropriate staff consultation.

While regular staff meetings are imperative, such meetings are difficult to arrange. It may be that attendance will vary from meeting to meeting, but with planned communication everyone will have a sense of being part of shared decisions and policies. Shared decision making is one of the most important elements in preventing staff burnout, along with providing variety in job tasks and small breaks during the day.

STAFF MEETINGS

1) Staff meetings should have a clear goal (clear purpose), a good agenda, and a good summary, and should be respectful of staff time. Start and end staff meetings on time. Lateness is not a virtue and busyness is not an excuse.

2) Staff meetings should be carefully planned and coordinated by the director with specific goals and clear ground rules. If the meeting is for the director to make announcements, it should not be billed as a meeting for discussion and decision making. There should be enough time to cover all the topics and make sound decisions.

3) The total staff doesn't always have to be at meetings. Sometimes subjects concern only certain staff members (ordering kitchen supplies, changing use of ball boxes in older children's yard, etc.).

4) In the employment of staff there should be clear description of assignments and regular and mutual evaluation of each staff member including the director.

5) Define the purpose of the meeting: Is it to socialize, share information, make decisions, share announcements, plan for the future, evaluate the past? Each requires a different structure and a different amount of time.

6) Two important requirements: Time to plan the meeting and by whom; time to evaluate and summarize the meeting.

7) Staff includes everyone who contributes to the operation of the program. Most directly involved are the teachers and director but a full staff may also include the cook, custodian or housekeeper, secretary, nurse, bookkeeper. This means that there must be opportunities for everybody to be involved so that they may function as a team. Creative ways must be found for necessary communication to take place—scheduled meetings, printed schedules, workshops, memos, log books, employer recognition, notes of appreciation.

Staff Potluck

Staff potlucks can provide a welcome chance to socialize and exchange perceptions about children and program, a very necessary aspect of staff planning.

There are differences of opinion regarding staff meetings during paid staff time. Certainly such time is a core aspect of teachers' functioning, and meeting during time for which staff is paid places staff work and planning in its proper, important place. Budgets should reflect this belief about the indispensable nature of staff exchange and planning.

Staff Development

Budgets should also reflect the importance of staff training. No matter how strong your staff, they can benefit from staff development on all kinds of topics. Ask your staff for their suggestions first, then follow through on them. Compensatory time off might be an appropriate way of acknowledging attendance at such meetings, if you are unable to provide for substitute coverage in your budget.

Such might also be the case with a one-day weekend staff retreat. It is usually impossible for the whole staff to take the day off together except on a weekend, but a yearly staff retreat can be a revivifying and enriching experience for all. This could be a day devoted to long-range planning and to plotting future directions for the program. It strengthens your plans and your program for everyone to be part of this process. It could be a time of evaluation, as well—reviewing your staff recruitment and selection process, having staff evaluate with you their success in achieving their individual goals and objectives—and for general brainstorming in all areas. Plan an agenda, but leave time open as well.

Using Community Resources

Some programs have been able to work out ways of using community resources to enrich their own understanding of children (see Chapter 16). The local Mental Health Association may offer consultation. A professor at a university may be interested in placing field-work students in the program for their learning and, in exchange, might hold a seminar or provide consultation on particular concerns. Community organizations such as the Family Service Association of America will be pleased to form an alliance out of concern for the same families they are serving in different ways. The local public health agencies will be delighted to serve program families and to enter into joint programs with them. Staff meetings could be organized intermittently to introduce these services and resources to staff.

*　　*　　*

It is important to remember that all the activities described in this book will be valuable in direct proportion to the amount of staff thinking and planning that goes on in tune with knowledge about and understanding of the children in the program and their parents. Sharing this knowledge and understanding will keep the partnership between parents and staff alive and strong.

Resources

Briggs, D.C. *Your Child's Self-Esteem.* Garden City, N.Y.: Doubleday, 1975.

Croft, D.J. *Parents and Teachers: A Resource Book for Home, School, and Community Relations.* Belmont, Calif.: Wadsworth, 1979.

Dobson, J. *Dare to Discipline.* New York: Tyndale House, 1977.

Erikson, E. *Childhood and Society.* New York: Norton, 1964.

Furman, E. *Helping Young Children Grow: I Never Knew Parents Did So Much.* Madison, Conn.: International Universities Press, 1987.

Ginott, H. *Between Parent and Child.* New York: Macmillan, 1965.

Gordon, I.J., and Breivogel, W.F., eds. *Building Effective Home School Relationships.* Boston: Allyn and Bacon, 1976.

Gordon, T. *Teacher Effectiveness Training.* New York: McKay, 1975.

Hymes, J.L., Jr. *Effective Home-School Relations* (rev. ed.). Carmel, Calif.: Hacienda Press, 1975.

Leach, P. *The Child Care Encyclopedia.* New York: Knopf, 1984.

Lyons, P., Robbins, A., and Smith, A. *Involving Parents: A Handbook for Participation in Schools.* Ypsilanti, Mich.: High/Scope, 1983.

Neugebauer, R., ed. *The Director's Magazine.* Redmond, Wash.: Child Care Information Exchange.

Stone, J.G. *Teacher-Parent Relationships.* Washington, D.C.: National Association for the Education of Young Children, 1987.

Wells, G. Talking With Children: The Complementary Roles of Parents and Teachers. In M. Donaldson, R. Grieve, and C. Pratt (eds.), *Early Childhood Development and Education* (pp. 127–150). New York: Guilford Press, 1983.

Extending Into the Community 16

The school-age program can be extended and enriched by a variety of community resources. Some of the community organizations and agencies through which children may pursue their interests are: Parks and Recreation Departments; local colleges and universities; Girl Scouts; Boy Scouts; Campfire; 4-H Clubs; special interest clubs and service organizations; Big Brothers and Sisters; dance and aerobics classes; and public libraries. You may also find that the Y programs or Boys' and Girls' Clubs offer activities that interest your children. In some cases, you may wish to team up with their after-school programs for special field trips or activities. This could happen when the cost of the activity is too high for one program, but manageable when two or three participate. Such might be the case for a special show at the local planetarium, for example.

Many communities, especially those with large immigrant populations, have a variety of associations and activity centers that reflect the community's ethnic cultures. These can be both a source of enrichment for the pro-

gram and a link to family values and interests. Staff need to acquaint themselves with the activities offered and with the culture's points of view.

The child enrolled in an extended-day program can participate in a wide array of after-school activities, just as any school-age child does. These activities, away from the home and the program, assume increasingly greater importance as children grow older. They provide children with opportunities to learn new skills and meet new people. It is important for children in an extended-day program to play with children other than those enrolled in that program and for your children to feel they are part of the same kind of after-school activities as their school friends, especially during summers and other vacation times. After-school activities away from the program also give children a needed opportunity to be independent and self-sufficient.

Making arrangements for children to go to after-school activities outside the program benefits both the children who leave and the children who remain in the program. Those

staying have more opportunity for small-group activities and for private chats with adult leaders. Look to the community as an established extension of your child care program. You will be able to increase the variety of experiences you offer to the children, thus enriching your children's lives and your program.

One of your best community resources is your local library. If you are lucky enough to have a children's librarian, get in touch and become familiar with what the library has to offer. Today, you'll find you can rent films, videocassettes, and records as well as borrow books. Sometimes libraries will arrange special story hours just for your children. If your library does not have a children's librarian, ask for the name of the children's specialist in your area's library system and work with that person.

Several important points must be considered when community resources are used to enrich a program. As a first step toward extending the after-school program into the community, the program must find out what

85

community resources are available. This means visiting agencies that offer programs for youth, talking with directors of those programs about whether your children can participate, observing these programs in action, and talking with the parents of the children enrolled. The staff should also establish standards that it feels programs should meet in order for them to be included. The ability and background of the teaching staff, the quality of the program, and how well the programs suit the individual child should all be considered in your decision.

If the community itself is viewed as an extension of the center, the variety of experiences offered through the center will be limited only by the number of different opportunities in the community and the effectiveness of the staff in finding ways for children to participate.

FIELD TRIPS

One of the simplest ways to tap into community resources is through field trips. These provide excellent opportunities for the children to get to know new and different parts of their community. Sometimes they can lead to long-term relationships as when program children help out in stores or work as volunteers in preschools or senior citizen centers. Almost any destination will do if you have planned carefully and checked arrangements thoroughly with people at the field trip site.

Simple Field Trips

These can be walks in your program's neighborhood, when you tape different sounds, make a list of different colors and smells, feel different textures, learn names of different plants and draw a picture of each different leaf, or write down different car makes and state license plates.

Field Visits

Take trips to local businesses and shops. For many children a trip to the market is great fun, especially if you are buying food for a cooking project. Children like to visit dry cleaners, delicatessens, bakeries, ice cream stores, health food stores, video rental stores, fire and police stations, newspaper offices, print shops, radio and TV stations, all kinds of repair shops, shopping malls (a special favorite with older children in the group), and even hospitals and pharmacies.

Because children are so concerned with what is "real," a visit to a gas station or any similar service location can be the highlight of a child's week.

Bus Trips

These trips require more advance preparation. Phone the bus company, ask them about the best time for the trip, and describe your plans based on the information they give you. If you are visiting a museum, airport, zoo, or special resource in your community, make sure those whom you are visiting have a clear idea of what you expect from them, when you plan to be there, and how many children you are bringing.

This is especially important when you are planning to visit centers with seniors or young children. Would the seniors like to see a talent show? How can your children be helpful to the preschool? Make sure everyone is clear on all aspects of the visit. Seniors might visit your program to help the children learn skills such as special sewing stitches or, perhaps, even to help with homework. Preschoolers love to visit school-age programs where the outdoor space is generally larger and where there are so many new and interesting things to see indoors. Visiting preschoolers give school-agers themselves a chance to act as big brothers and big sisters.

Colleges, Community Colleges, and Universities

These institutions can be a tremendous resource for your program. Find out when you can use their athletic facilities or their kiln. See if your children can attend a rehearsal of a play the students are performing. Visit their art gallery, or their zoology and biology departments. Find out if their students are interested in volunteering in your program. See if they have an extension or community outreach program through which a professor might offer a short course to your students on your site. Such institutions can prove to be your greatest community resource.

It is really important to keep in mind what you can offer the places you visit. Use of community resources should not be a one-way street. What can your children do for those at the field trip site? It can be as simple as an attractive thank-you letter that a merchant can put up on the wall, or it can be gifts the children make for their senior citizen friends. Children need to learn to be "givers" as well as "takers."

Rules

Be sure all members of your group have a clear idea of the rules of the trip; discuss them thoroughly before you leave your site. Such basics as staying on the sidewalk and crossing the street as a group need to be said many times to school-agers. If you are going someplace such as a convalescent home where special behavior is required, talk about how the children will be expected to act and practice in a couple of role-playing sessions. Don't take a group with more children than you feel comfortable about and be sure you always have a small first aid kit with you. And last but not least, have fun!

Parents

Parents must be free to decide whether they wish their children to participate. Permission slips for all activities are essential. Parents and staff must decide together what is right for each individual child. If a parent wishes to enroll a child in a special program, it is preferable for parents to make these arrangements themselves.

HELPING FAMILIES

Other community resources help families too. You should be familiar with whatever is available in the community and be able to judge when families may need help from these agencies. You should know what procedures need to be followed for referrals and what the financial and eligibility requirements of each agency are. Some parents who use extended-day programs are struggling with various health, social welfare, legal, and financial problems. You and your staff should establish communication with those community agencies that deal with the problems faced by parents. This is especially important for anything that may be related to child abuse. You and your staff need to know state laws regarding reporting procedures and you should be familiar with such programs as Parents Anonymous. You also need to be aware of local drug abuse programs for both adults and children.

Some programs have found ways of bringing services to the program through on-site visits and consultation at hours when parents bring or pick up their children. Parents are able to meet with a family counselor who can assist them in dealing with their problems or help them find the right agency from which to seek help. Community agencies can sometimes provide such a service.

The following agencies may be helpful in establishing communication: Family Service Association of America, Jewish Family Service, Visiting Nurses' Association, Catholic Social Service, Child Protective Service Agency, Department of Health Services, Probation Department, Department of Rehabilitation, Community Family Health Centers, the Dental Society, and Mental Health Centers. Rotary, Lions, Kiwanis, and other service clubs may also prove to be helpful to your program.

Liaison between extended-day programs and elementary schools is especially important. Because the school and the program share responsibility for children, channels of communication should be established and kept open so that the school and the program respect each other's contribution to the child's life. Many times working parents' schedules prevent them from attending school functions or meeting school personnel firsthand. You can become a bridge between families and the school, interpreting policy decisions, explaining procedures and schedules, and translating sometimes confusing messages relayed by your younger children. If your children regularly write reports for homework, ask their classroom teacher if they can do reports on trips with you. Use any way possible to develop good relationships with the classroom teachers. Some will view your programs primarily as a good place for their students to do their homework; invite them in and show off your program. Remember, through joint efforts, school and extended-day care can supplement each other's important contributions to the lives of children and families.

INDEX

Information About NAEYC

NAEYC is . . .

. . . a membership-supported organization of people committed to fostering the growth and development of children from birth through age 8. Membership is open to all who share a desire to serve and act on behalf of the needs and rights of young children.

NAEYC provides . . .

. . . educational services and resources to adults who work with and for children, including

- **Young Children,** *the* journal for early childhood educators
- **Books, posters, brochures** and **videos** to expand your professional knowledge and commitment to young children, with topics including infants, curriculum, research, discipline, teacher education, and parent involvement
- An **Annual Conference** that brings people from all over the country to share their expertise and advocate on behalf of children and families

- **Week of the Young Child** celebrations sponsored by NAEYC Affiliate Groups across the nation to call public attention to the needs and rights of children and families
- **Insurance plans** for individuals and programs
- **Public affairs information** for knowledgeable advocacy efforts at all levels of government and through the media
- The **National Academy of Early Childhood Programs,** a voluntary accreditation system for high-quality programs for young children
- The **Information Service,** a centralized source of information sharing, distribution, and collaboration

For **free** information about membership, publications, or other NAEYC services . . .

. . . **call** NAEYC 202-232-8777 or 800-424-2460 or **write to** NAEYC, 1834 Connecticut Avenue, N.W., Washington, DC 20009-5786.